Praise for Spiritual Connection in Daily Life

"This is the best book available today for anyone of us who feel the need to transform our lives. Over many years, Lynn Underwood quietly developed what is now internationally renowned as the most thoughtful and valid measure of spirituality available today. The reader will find opportunity for deepened self-awareness and spiritual growth in responding to each question, and will find that this spiritual classic and powerful self-assessment tool opens up new horizons of serenity, hope, joy, and vision. Its scientific grounding is impeccable."
—STEPHEN G. POST, PhD, professor of preventive medicine, Stony Brook University

"Grounded in science and authentic personal experience, this book is a treasure of profound wisdom. Everyone can benefit from deepening awareness of their own spirituality by reflecting on these questions and learning how others have responded. The book is an inspiring gift of love made visible." —FRANCES VAUGHAN, PhD, psychologist and author, *Shadows of the Sacred*

"Lynn Underwood's *Spiritual Connection in Daily Life* is a welcome and valuable contribution for caregivers, professionals, patients, and ordinary people. She creates a pluralistic approach rich in stories and examples from around the world, yet grounded in research. The author encourages readers to explore their experiences of love and connections to people, the universe, and God (or the holy or divine) and to use her questions as a starting point for discussion and reflection rather than a conclusion." —RABBI ROBERT TABAK, staff chaplain at the Hospital of the University of Pennsylvania

"I warmly recommend this practical exercise for establishing one's personal spiritual profile—its strengths, and its, as yet, unfulfilled potential. Particularly valuable are the insights arising as to how one might progress towards an enhanced relationship with God and with

D1057283

other people, as well as have a greater awareness of all that life has to offer." —RUSSELL STANNARD, emeritus professor of physics, Open University, U.K.

"Through her Daily Spiritual Experience Scale, Lynn Underwood has elegantly bridged a divide between science and spirituality in language and experiences that are accessible to all religions, faith traditions, and cultures. This book is not just for reading; it is for experiencing and savoring. It is rich food for the soul." —THE REV. WALTER J. SMITH, SJ, PHD, president and CEO, HealthCare Chaplaincy

"As a scholar in the field of traumatic stress I always encourage my students to look beyond the impact of stressful events into the realm of human nature resilience. My research has shown me that Underwood's Daily Spiritual Experience Scale is an important measurement that taps the unique experience of spirituality as it is manifested in day-to-day life. I would recommend this book to managers of stressful work places who are interested in promoting the well-being of their workers."
—GADI ZERACH, PHD, clinical psychologist, Department of Behavioral Sciences, Ariel University, Israel

"*Spiritual Connection in Daily Life* introduces a remarkable concept known as the Daily Spiritual Experience Scale, which consists of sixteen multiple-choice questions measuring among other things your daily life connections with others, divine providence, your inner spirit, and nature. This scale helps us find the "spiritual connection" in one's daily life and one's sense of compassion, love, joy, and inner peace. An excellent tool." —DR. ALWI SHIHAB, Islamic scholar, trustee, University of Indonesia, Jakarta, and Hartford Seminary

Dear Nan
I hope you like this. Sixty years ago we had our introductory blind date when I asked Susie Allen to find me a woman "who talked about God at dep parties"
Happy Birthday
Love George

Spiritual Connection in Daily Life

Spiritual
CONNECTION
in Daily Life

**SIXTEEN LITTLE QUESTIONS
THAT CAN MAKE
A BIG DIFFERENCE**

Lynn Underwood

TEMPLETON PRESS

Templeton Press
300 Conshohocken State Road, Suite 500
West Conshohocken, PA 19428
www.templetonpress.org

Designed by Gopa & Ted2, Inc.

Cover art and interior images © Lynn Underwood

Permissions Acknowledgments
Excerpt from "Had I Not Been Awake," from *The Human Chain,* by Seamus
Heaney Copyright © 2010 by Seamus Heaney. Reprinted by permission of
Farrar, Straus, and Giroux, LLC and Faber and Faber.

Excerpt from "Postscript" from *The Spirit Level* by Seamus Heaney.
Copyright © 1996 by Seamus Heaney. Reprinted by permission of Farrar
Straus and Giroux, LLC and Faber and Faber.

"The One" by Patrick Kavanagh is reprinted from *Collected Poems*
(Allen Lane, 2004) by kind permission of the Trustees of the Estate of the late
Katherine B. Kavanagh, through the Jonathan Williams Literary Agency.

Permission was graciously granted to use an excerpt from the Rumi poem,
"Some Kiss We Want," by the translator, Coleman Barks.

Permission to use the translation of Rainer Maria Rilke's "Gott spricht zu
jedem nur, eh er ihn macht," was granted by the translator, Eric Beversluis.

The excerpt from the poem, "God the Eater" by Stevie Smith, from the
Collected Poems of Stevie Smith, copyright ©1972 by Stevie Smith is reprinted
by permission of New Directions Publishing Corp, and by permission of
the Estate of James MacGibbon.

Excerpt from "Any Morning," by William Stafford is Copyright © 1993
by William Stafford and is used with the permission of The Permissions
Company, Inc., on behalf of The Estate of William Stafford.

Library of Congress Cataloging-in-Publication Data on file.

Printed in the United States of America

13 14 15 16 17 18   10 9 8 7 6 5 4 3 2 1

Contents

PART ONE
Why Read This Book?

1 Invitation and Introduction

Everyone takes the limits of his own vision for the
limits of the world.
—ARTHUR SCHOPENHAUER

What does the world look like to you? What is the
texture of your daily life? Do you find richness, jazz,
color, deep satisfaction? Or do you often feel swamped
by discouragement, apathy, stress, exhaustion? Where do you look
to relieve dullness or distress if and when it plagues you? I often
find myself looking for solace and stimulation in food and drink,
using the computer, buying things, working obsessively, or looking
for entertaining distractions. We have superficial social encoun-
ters, in person or electronically, that do not really provide the deep
connection we are looking for. At other times we just settle into a
lull of complacent boredom. We deal.

There are sources of experience that can add vibrant flavor
that doesn't fade, providing a renewable inner resource. These
can include being spiritually touched by the beauty of nature, the
wow of a sunset. We can give and receive love, or feel thankful
for our blessings. We can experience deep peacefulness or find
spiritual strength in the midst of stressful times. We can sense the
presence of God, or the divine. These ordinary experiences of the
"more than," the transcendent, can add punch to our days. They

can transform a dull day into one full of light. This book explores ways to draw our attention to these experiences, to cultivate awareness of flavors that are already there in daily life, but that we are somehow missing.

There are times when we feel fully alive. There are other times when life feels flat. It is not always the obviously exciting times that make us feel fully alive. In times of quiet contentment or even times of engaged struggle we can feel awake to the richness of life. We say something kind to someone and see his face light up. A child gives us an exuberant hug. We smell bread baking in our mother's kitchen. We hear the waves on the beach. We experience a tough situation and are not pulled under by it. During moments like these, the rough and the smooth, we can sometimes sense a kind of timelessness. We may also sense that something is happening that has profound significance, significance beyond this moment.

What you bring to your ways of perceiving the events of your days is so important to the color, the flavor, the texture that you find. What do you look for, what do you expect, and what do you find as you go through each day? So often we can become hypnotized by a vision of the mundane details of life as boring, senseless, or pointless. Are your lenses clouded by this hypnotic view? Are your taste buds dulled? If that is the case, you can miss the beauty, joy, and vibrancy that are there not only in the obviously happy times, but also in the midst of suffering and struggle.

In the interests of cultivating this ability to appreciate and sense the "more than" in the midst of your days, and to communicate about this with others if you want to, this book offers a set of sixteen questions. Each question is designed to draw attention to a particular aspect of life, providing both an opportunity for enrichment and flourishing, and a common language to communicate experiences that may otherwise be difficult to share. We can become more alive together. These simple multiple-choice questions form the Daily Spiritual Experience Scale.

The spiritual experiences that these sixteen questions measure are not exotic, like near-death experiences or hearing voices, or dramatic religious conversion, but ordinary experiences that many people of many different beliefs and cultures have. Overall, these are good feelings that lift us up, but they can also challenge us. They provide an internal source of zip, aliveness, jazz, a sustaining buzz that can also nourish us over the long haul. We often think it is the big things in life that are most important, but our lives are actually made up of many small moments that contribute to the rich texture of each day. We sometimes underestimate the contribution this texture and substance make to the big picture, but without them there is no big picture.

Tens of thousands of people have answered the questions in the Daily Spiritual Experience Scale. All kinds of people, from a wide variety of cultures and countries, use the questions for various purposes: doctors, psychologists, ministers, teachers, nurses, managers, social workers, chaplains, and students. Since I developed the scale, they contact me frequently and I read the published articles describing the results of research using the scale. I get involved in the research and the translations. But what I enjoy most is how the individual questions help people to think in a focused way about these experiences of the "more than" in their daily lives—how the questions help people identify underlying things of importance. And how the questions can enhance communication, enabling people to better understand one another. Rather than leading us to quibble over how each of us defines *spirituality*, these questions focus on the specifics such as awe, gratitude, other-centered love, and sense of connection. This set of questions, which has been useful in research and therapy, can be useful on a personal level, too.

A More Satisfying Life

Many people find that ordinary spiritual experiences are part of a more satisfying life. This is true for those who call themselves religious as well as for those who would say they were not religious. In research using the questions in a variety of settings throughout the world, scores on the Daily Spiritual Experience Scale (DSES) have been linked to many good things in life, such as increased happiness, shorter hospital stays, better health behaviors, weight loss, diminished pain, recovery from addictions, and prevention of burnout. More frequent experiences as reported using the Daily Spiritual Experience Scale tend to predict better outcomes of various kinds. These kinds of experiences can also, in and of themselves, improve life's quality, make life more worth living. They can also act as signals that we are heading in the right direction as we make decisions in our lives.

These spiritual experiences can also help us to stick with activities that enable us to flourish, such as prayer or meditation, taking time in nature, or engaging in activities that nurture others. In the process we may become more fully ourselves and more fully alive. People often find that they have more of these experiences in the midst of dire circumstances, or as they cope with difficult situations. This may be because these kinds of spiritual experiences give us refreshing food that can help to sustain us in difficult times.

In this book I am sharing experiences from my own life and experiences of others as well as scientific exploration. But most of all I am inviting you to engage in a way that hopefully enhances your sense of the real on a daily basis and improves the quality of your life. My hope is that this book will help you to have a more delightful and grounded life. As you enhance your abilities to see spiritual connection in your life, you can get more in touch with what is real in a more complex and accurate way.

Management seminars and books warn against letting the "urgent" drive out the "important." We find ourselves prioritizing what is urgent and forgetting about what is important. We miss the spiritual elements of daily life because we are too busy attending to other things. Measuring our Daily Spiritual Experiences, and learning about those of others, can draw attention to things that we may have moved to the back burner, or even off the stove altogether, in response to the pressing urgencies of life. Meanwhile, we return to the stove and find that we have no sauce and vegetables, just white rice and boiled water.

The editor of *Poetry* magazine recently wrote,

> It is as if each of us were always hearing some strange, complicated music in the background of our lives, music which, so long as it remains in the background, is not simply distracting but manifestly unpleasant, because it demands the attention we are giving to other things. It is not hard to hear this music, but it is very difficult indeed to learn to hear it as music.[1]

Is there music in your life that you are missing?

Answering the DSES Questions Can Change Us

Raising awareness by answering the questions in this book can change the way we see each day, and change us in the process.

As we consider our answers, it can help us to be on the lookout for these experiences, savoring them when they occur. The term *subconscious* lost favor with the decline of Freud's theories, but "implicit" knowledge is a hot term in neuroscience and psychology today. *Implicit* refers to those things we are not aware of but which can "drive the bus" of our actions and attitudes. Answering questions can powerfully drag things from implicit to explicit—out into the open. In the process, we become more aware of things that were under the surface, unacknowledged. A friend of mine in the marketing field recently said, "Attention is our most valuable resource." Marketers want to grab this valuable resource. But we can take control of our attention instead of letting others control it. We can pay attention to those things that will truly enhance our lives and deserve our attention. Here are some examples of how this can happen as you go through this book:

- Good feelings in life powerfully lift us up, even more than negative things drag us down.[2] So rather than squashing down the negative things, or trying to talk ourselves out of them, increasing our positive feelings is the more effective strategy. Answering the sixteen questions in this book can do just that by calling our attention to these positive experiences and exploring ways to find more of them.
- We filter the world emotionally on a moment-to-moment basis. These filters in turn shape our ultimate moods, feelings, and understandings.[3] Answering the DSES questions can adjust our emotional filters to allow in more light.
- Even if we are not explicitly aware of things, they can have "priming" effects on our lives. Words, touch, smells, and music affect our behaviors in ways that we are not aware of. As we bring attention to the aspects of the "more than" in life by answering the DSES questions, subliminal yet

positive effects on life occur over time.[4]

- Even a few minutes of expressive writing has been shown to improve mental and physical health.[5] In this book you have lots of chances to write expressively about your life in response to the questions, and you are challenged to do that repeatedly. Putting feelings into words can also help us to manage negative feelings, a process that works at the level of brain structures.[6] Savoring positive events promotes positive feelings, and telling others about these can increase our overall satisfaction with life.[7] You have the opportunity to do this as you answer the questions yourself, and, as suggested in Chapter 10, you have the opportunity to increase this satisfaction by sharing with others.

There are many reasons why the process of reading this book and answering the questions, and then revisiting them again over time, will be good for you. But I also want this book to be fun, like playing a game. I hope that this book will add both spice and a healing balm to your life.

Enhancing Our Sensitivities Rather Than Stifling Our Feelings

Some of us are more sensitive than others. We feel pain more strongly, we are more aware of loneliness or alienation, we feel the joys of life more intensely. On the one hand, this kind of sensitivity can be something we would rather not have. On the other hand, this same sensitivity might enable us to find spiritual experiences more easily.

We all have the basic capacity to feel all sorts of things in life. We may cut ourselves off from our sensitivities because we are afraid of being hurt. Seeking to numb ourselves from pain, we may also cut ourselves off from the ability to perceive transcendent joys. Because uplifting moments, rather than the downers, are more important in predicting happiness, this is not such a good idea.[8] Negative feelings are part and parcel of life, but we may forget that they are just not as important to the big picture. Of course, we do not seek out painful experiences, but pain is part of life and can be informative. We may need to experience the pain of a person's absence, for example, in order to fully appreciate the person when he or she is with us. Even though suffering is unavoidable, spiritual experiences can mitigate its negative effects.

We can cultivate certain kinds of sensitivities. When I read the reports of wine experts, I know that I do not have these subtle sensations. On the other hand, I respond to certain kinds of music in ways that others miss. Artistic and musical sensibilities, like wine sensibility, can be cultivated. These can really enrich life. What kinds of sensitivities do our particular cultural environments discourage or encourage? Can we also do things to cultivate our sensitivity to spiritual experiences?

Rather than numbing the system with superficial stimuli—alcohol, surfing the Web, shopping, eating, video games—how about giving the sensitive system a chance to be just that—sensitive? Then we can enjoy what is there to be enjoyed, no matter what the circumstances.

Seamus Heaney, the Nobel Prize–winning poet, does a great job of alerting us to all that we might miss if we forget to pay attention to all that is embedded in our daily lives.

> Had I not been awake I would have missed it,
> A wind that rose and whirled until the roof
> Pattered with quick leaves off the sycamore

And got me up, the whole of me a-patter,
Alive and ticking like an electric fence:
Had I not been awake I would have missed it. . . .[9]

By drawing attention to particular things in your day as you answer the questions in this book, you can increase your sensitivity to various aspects of life. The kinds of experiences others describe can also wake up your sensitivities as you read about them. The arts, humor, and other resources can also help to wake up your sensitivity to the "more than" in life, providing you with microscopes and telescopes to enhance your abilities to see more clearly.

Enhancing Communication and Relationships

The more we truly understand each other, the better our relationships. The more we understand about each other, the more we can learn from each other. Each of us is unique, including a particular combination of background, sensitivities, personality, culture, and reaction to religious thought and practice. The Daily Spiritual Experience Scale can provide ways to communicate by offering a structured starting point for discussion. Your descriptions of your particular experiences and your report of how often you have these experiences both reveal something about you and how you function. The fact that there are no "right" answers helps this process. You can also share with others the kinds of resources, environments, and activities that are connected with these experiences in your life. Discussion of the questions and your answers can open understanding, provide mutual enrichment, and enhance the basis of relationships.

How and Why Was the Daily Spiritual Experience Scale Developed? What Does Science Contribute?

Not all real things are obvious. A microscope can make us aware of germs, and therefore be more cautious of them. A scientific study can reveal some pattern that was previously unseen.

I ended up studying spiritual experience as a scientist because I thought it was a very important part of life that was being left out of health and social scientific studies. I tried to measure it, in order to make it part of the mix in health and social science research, where things need to be assigned a number to be included. In a structured way, I composed a "measurement tool," something like a microscope or a telescope, but with words. The wording of the questions provides a lens to bring experiences into focus. I have been surprised at how much this set of sixteen questions is now being used throughout the world. It has already been translated into more than twenty-five languages. By scientific standards it "works," meaning that it predicts some things, is correlated with some things, and has mathematical and statistical validity, using psychometric tools.

I used scientific methods to develop the Daily Spiritual Experience Scale (DSES) so that it would reflect not just my experiences, but those of many others with different takes on life. Scientists try, as much as possible, to take the perspective of a "neutral" person, to remove biases as we look at problems. This has been crucial in the success of the DSES, and has made it useful across religious and cultural divides. Like any scientific measurement tool, such as a thermometer or a microscope, it has its limits, but it can provide a concrete basis for communication as well as research. Each of us is unique in our background, our relationship to or estrangement from religious thought and practices, our culture.

This measurement tool—with its scientific basis—can provide a way to communicate between very different people, a point to start discussion.

When scientists develop questionnaires in the social and medical sciences, we start with our own experiences and those of people we know, as well as with various assumptions. This happens with topics ranging from the level of pain people are experiencing to how stressed out they feel. This is not an awful starting point, but if we stop there we limit the questionnaire's usefulness. People's experiences of pain, stress, and social relationships differ so much. In developing the DSES, while diving into the depths of my own spiritual experiences to get at the things of interest, I also explored various theological and philosophical roots and concepts. Most important, I talked to lots of different kinds of people and read widely beyond my comfort zone to find the variety of experiences out there, and to identify how language is used in different ways to identify those experiences.

You may wonder why there are sixteen questions. Questionnaires used for research and assessment cannot have too many questions or they are just too much of a burden. So the goal in designing this scale was to have as few questions as possible, but still address the breadth of qualities and give space for variety. In some ways the scale measures one thing—spiritual connection—but in other ways it measures sixteen specific kinds of things, each question getting at a special kind of spiritual connection that people reported as being important, and that research and theory supported. This limited number of questions makes it manageable for you, too, as you work through this book.

I am using the Daily Spiritual Experience Scale to provide the backbone for this book, so that you can engage in a process that is both fun and useful. You can answer these sixteen questions and see how your answers change over time. You can share your responses with others, if you want to. There are no "right" or "better" answers. It is more like a personality test that reveals something about you and how you function. Each of us is unique, and each of our experiences is unique. However, scientific measurement can help to provide a way to compare our experiences with those of others to some extent. And it can provide a common language to communicate with others.

This book uses each of the DSES questions with its multiple-choice response set as a place to start. But you are also invited to explore the quality, the particulars, of your experiences. You then have the option of looking at your number scores in various ways or never doing anything with the number scores beyond your initial responses to the sixteen questions in Chapter 3. You can benefit from the book no matter which you choose.

The scientists who have used this scale in research accept that these experiences are real from the point of view of those who answer the set of questions. They accept this even if they themselves do not personally believe that the answers reflect real connections. Many scientists and others who use the instrument do so because they see that these questions represent something important in the lives of those they work with. And they see that these experiences predict other things—they are practical. In this book we are remaining radically open to the possibility that something transcendent, something eternal, does exist, and that connecting with this in various ways has the capacity to improve our lives. The combination of radical openness with sharpening perception is an ideal of science. We are aiming for that here. Great science is radically open.

This book does not dwell on beliefs, but rather focuses on our experiences. You and I get tastes of transcendent connection in our daily lives. They seem coherent in some profound way, touching something within us that feels real. We sense that something of importance is found here. Where and when do you find these? What do these experiences tell you? How do they affect you? What do the experiences of others have to say that you find interesting? Do they open doors for you?

A Multicultural Meeting in Geneva, Switzerland

One of the most exciting times in my life was the time spent in meetings at the World Health Organization (WHO) with people from all over the world, and from all major religions as well as atheists and agnostics. We were discussing the meaning of the Daily Spiritual Experience questions in the context of a project I helped coordinate on "quality of life." The WHO wisely realized that just being physically or mentally sick or well did not adequately sum up quality of life for people, and that it was necessary to include aspects of spirituality in order to fully assess quality of life. During the course of the meetings, many focus groups were conducted in different countries to gather feedback from ordinary people living their lives with illness in different cultures. (The countries included China, India, Japan, Kenya, Brazil, Spain, Turkey, Israel, the United Kingdom, Sweden, Iran, Egypt, and others.) It was one of the most interesting projects I have ever been involved in. It helped shape the Daily Spiritual Experience Scale, and the questions from the scale also helped to inform that project.

I learned a lot at this meeting. I had great, long conversations and spent time together at meals and on walks with many delightful people. I discovered something that powerfully shaped my thinking. When I talked with those deeply living out their own faith tradition in a committed way with integrity, I was able to find common ground. I felt comfortable with them. I found I had more in common with many from very different religious and cultural backgrounds than I had with people at home, whom I would have considered more theologically similar to me. I don't think this reduces to "all religions are the same." But those who find deep roots, yet remain open-minded and aware of the limits of understanding, can make real connections with others, learn from them, and find value in other perspectives.

Putting the draft of the Daily Spiritual Experience questions on the table at meetings opened up conversation between people from diverse cultural orientations in a very concrete and enlivening way. It moved the conversation from beliefs to experiences, grounding conversation in the nitty-gritty of the daily. We may differ in our beliefs, but we can still have similar experiences, or share about different experiences using common language.

Passion and Neutrality

I have spent many years working with those in the scientific community and also with those of many faith traditions and those who have no affinity for traditional faith. I have had to write as inclusively as I can, while also trying to keep my own opinion out of the mix. But there is just no way for a human being to be completely neutral. A good scientist cannot pretend she has no opinions, but only hope that her opinions do not crowd out deeper understanding.

I may be trained as a scientist, and try to be analytic and neutral, but I also bring to the table my own perspective, opinions, and passions. They will seep out in this book. Just as scientific ways of thinking can contribute to a good conversation, sharing passions respectfully can create a better space for others to express themselves and their views. The things that appeal to me will rise to the surface in this book: my tastes in music, visual art, television and film, the religious and secular sources that have been helpful to me, the cultures I have benefited from. I will be drawing more on religious traditions I am most familiar with, but, hopefully, deep will call to deep, and those with different views and backgrounds will nevertheless find something to relate to.

The resources in this book have been enriched by my relationships with others—what excites them and inspires them. I hope that over time, on the Web or in additional writing, in conversations using the structure of the book and continual input from others, I can increase the variety of resources I draw from. My language continues to stretch, as the words and structures of others allow me to see more divine connection in many forms. But I strongly believe that our passion enables us to inspire one another.

What to Expect from the Rest of This Book

Part Two, "Exploring Your Experiences," begins with a brief set of guidelines and instructions for answering the sixteen multiple-choice DSES questions (Chapter 2). Then in Chapter 3, each of the questions is presented separately, and you have the opportunity to answer each, express your own ideas and feelings, and reflect on your own experiences in depth.

Part Three, "Why Numbers?," looks at the number scores in more detail. Chapter 4 asks, What do they mean? How do you interpret them? What can you do with them? In Chapter 5 you will find some results from the many research studies using the Daily Spiritual Experience Scale, summarizing the kinds of things in life the scores predict and some of the ways it is currently being used in research and practical settings. If you hate numbers or just do not find them helpful in this context, you can skip Part Three altogether and still benefit from the book.

Part Four, "Themes," invites you to explore and respond to underlying themes exposed by the Daily Spiritual Experience Scale. By examining themes you explore ways of integrating the questions into broader issues that you deal with in your life. You have the opportunity to do this in Chapter 6 on the flow of love, Chapter 7 on connection and alienation, and Chapter 8 on your reactions to the rough and smooth realities of your life. Part Four finishes with Chapter 9, where you have a chance to reflect on how you envision the divine in your life.

Part Five, "Springboard for Communication," describes practical ways to connect with other people using the DSES. Chapter 10 provides some guidelines for making the most of conversations using the questions, and Chapter 11 suggests how to use the scale to communicate in personal relationships, organizations, and therapeutic settings.

The final part—Part Six, "Awake and Alive"—describes ways to continue to find spiritual flavor in life. The book itself is a guide to becoming more aware of specific experiences and the themes that undergird some of them. You can try out some of the specific additional suggestions and see how they affect your answers to the questions—either the number scores or the descriptions of experiences in words.

There is also a website to accompany the book: www.spiritualconnectionindailylife.com.

My hope is that the ideas in this book can start out as a game, a kind of "Where's Waldo?" This can lead on to exploration, discovery, and sharing with others in more satisfying ways about things that are exciting, soothing, and important to us. We are looking for experiences that satisfy our deepest desires. Let's see what we can find.

Part Two

Exploring Your Experiences

2 Instructions for Answering the Sixteen Questions

You can observe a lot just by watching.
—YOGI BERRA, BASEBALL PLAYER

Before diving into answering the sixteen Daily Spiritual Experience Scale questions, this chapter gives some basic instructions. Although you will be assigning a number to each question according to how often you have specific experiences, more importantly you will be invited to describe specifically what it is that you experience, to unpack parts of your life. Each person's responses are unique. Your pulse comes from a unique heart. Your descriptions of your experiences come from a unique "you."

Just answering these questions and exploring these parts of your life can help you more easily find things like joy, loving connection, and deep peace in the midst of your days. But you will also find out more about yourself. Rather than just quickly taking the test, getting a score, and going on with the rest of life, we will be going more slowly, exploring how these items can get us more involved in the life we have, and, in that engagement, making it more flavorful. To do this we will be savoring the items. When researchers use them, each question is important in analyzing the results and figuring out what they all mean. And each question stimulates conversations with people on these topics in the process. You are going to do this with yourself—do research on yourself, get a conversation going with yourself.

Answering the sixteen questions using the multiple-choice scores translates a complex part of your life into a set of numbers. This allows all sorts of statistical analyses to be done, which can be useful. But the numbers are a crude measurement—they cannot tap into the subtleties of your own particular experience. There are some gains and some losses in assigning number scores. Giving something a number provides an anchor for exploring our experiences. It distills the subtleties in a way that helps us to begin to learn from others and discuss things with them. Numbers give us a way of counting things and sorting them, putting them into buckets. It also lets us compare scores *with ourselves* over time. Later, in Chapter 4, you can examine the numbers, the scores, and use the numbers as a tool. But remember, the goal is not to get the highest possible score. Human spirituality is very complex and certainly includes more than these experiences. The DSES is not like an exam, where higher scores would mean you are necessarily more spiritual. Nevertheless, the scores do tell you something about your own spiritual experiences, and through the book you will discover more about what these might mean for you.

Finding Things in Your Personal Jungle

To get beyond the limits of a numerical score, we will use something that scientists call *qualitative* methods. Anthropologists were the first to use this "softer" scientific approach to understanding people very different from themselves. For example, they would spend time with people living deep in a jungle area, asking them questions to find out about their attitudes and relationships, and recording rich descriptions of their daily lives. We do something like this in everyday conversation when we ask our friends open-ended questions; we want to better understand how they see things and feel. We do it "scientifically" when we don't lead the person being questioned to the answers we might want to hear, and when we ask questions that get at exactly what we are interested in. For example, asking "How are you?" often leads to the response, "Fine." This is usually not the best way to find out how the person is really doing. The way we ask a question can affect the answer we get, what we learn. In this part of the book you will have the opportunity to ask yourself open-ended questions as if you were an anthropologist, trying to get an accurate answer that describes things as they are. Traveling into your own jungle.

When I developed the Daily Spiritual Experience questions, I used structured interviews, a kind of qualitative method, to ask a set of open-ended questions about ordinary experiences. That helped me refine my search for just the right questions to get at spiritual experiences of many kinds and finalize the categories. You will find results from these interviews sprinkled throughout the book. The kinds of people I included in the original development and testing included college students, nine- to fifteen-year-olds, young and older people, and people from many different religious, ethnic, and social groups in the United States. I did interviews with sick people. I interviewed Trappist (Cistercian) Christian monks and a selection of Benedictine monks. Due to their training in motivational insight, and the effect of their spiritual discipline on awareness and mindfulness, I found their insights particularly helpful. Some responses from Muslim Afghan refugees are included as well. Then, while organizing and participating in two working groups that gathered for World Health Organization projects, I had a great interviewing opportunity. The meetings included people from twenty-five countries (including Egypt, Sweden, the

United Kingdom, Turkey, China, Brazil, Spain, Israel, Kenya, Australia, and Japan) and from all major religious as well as indigenous and other more minor traditions, agnostics, and atheists.

For me the most exciting thing about the interviews was that I got to know so much about each of these people and the breadth of their spiritual experiences, and through this I got to know them more intimately. I continue to do interviews today, and they continue to stretch my understanding. These conversations still bring me joy.

Guidelines before You Dive into the Questions

The Introductory Statements Are Important

I don't read instructions. I avoid them if at all possible. I have had an Apple laptop computer since 1992, and one reason for this is that I find it easier to just intuit my way into new programs and systems and Apple has been friendly to this approach. I figure that if I cannot use a piece of equipment without instructions, it just is not worth it. But this has not always worked.

It is important to read the following brief introductory sentences of the DSES carefully before diving into the individual items. The introduction to this scale is part of the scale, and vital to the questions working well for many people, maybe even more so for those inclined not to read the instructions. Here it is broken down into its two main parts.

No Judging

The first part of the instruction reads,

> The list that follows includes items you may or may not experience. Please consider how often you directly have

this experience, and try to disregard whether you feel you should or should not have these experiences.

This reminds you that there are no universally "right" answers, no "better" scores. Some people will never have some of these experiences, and that is just fine. This scale is not designed to measure how spiritual you are. It measures how frequently you have specific kinds of ordinary spiritual experiences. Some items may resonate with you; others may not. This may change over time. A higher total score doesn't mean you are more spiritual. Answer just as things are for you, without judging yourself.

Later you will have a chance to consider which of the items are most important to you, and which ones you might especially wish to find more of in your life. But for now, just observe and reflect, enjoying the spectrum of flavors in your life as you find them.

Divine, Holy, Transcendent

The second part of the introduction is,

> A number of items use the word *God*. If this word is not a comfortable one for you, please substitute another word which calls to mind the divine or holy for you.

You want to answer the questions in a way that best fits your relationship with the divine. Half of the questions in the DSES use the word *God*. In this book I explicitly give a possible alternative wording for each of those items, but these suggestions do not exhaust the possibilities.

The word *God* has such different meanings for different people. Some people are alienated from traditional religions, and they have a negative reaction to the word *God*. My response to the word

God has changed over time. Earlier in my life the combination of the word *God* and the pronoun *he* was deadly, referring to some frowning father figure with expectations too high for me ever to reach. The image of an old white man with a beard on a cloud does not agree with the divine presence in any mature faith tradition that I am aware of. When I designed these questions, I was trying to get at some basic experiences of relationship with the divine. The word *God* helps many to identify these experiences; it gets in the way for others. That is the reason for the option to substitute a different word in the instructions at the beginning of the scale, and the suggestions for alternate wording.

Transcendent is a word I like, but it does not work for everyone. Most spiritual systems have a sense of the "more than." For many this is a personal divine being. A Native American adaptation of the scale substituted the word *Creator*[1] for *God*. A translation adapted for Afghan refugees in the United States replaced the word *God* with *Allah*.[2] Some orthodox Jews are most comfortable with *G-d*. Those of you who find another word that works better for you could actually cross out *God*, and write that word in its place.

I wanted this scale to be able to reach those who were not comfortable with the word *God*, but I also realized that for those who believe in a god, and even for some who say they do not, the word *God* is often the best pointer. In my extensive interviews while developing the scale, the word *God* captured the experience of relating to the transcendent, especially with the substitution option presented in the introduction. For example, focus groups addressing this issue were conducted with inner-city African American adolescents in an alcoholism risk-behavior study. In response to the use of the term *higher power* in place of *God* in the questions, both the religious and the nonreligious members of the group asked, "Do you mean God? Then why not just say it?"[3] For many, God is not higher, or a power, but more a divine partner in life's challenges, even if a more powerful partner.

Ultimately, the concept of the divine is ineffable for most people; we just cannot express it in a single word or phrase. But rather than using a concept that is too broad and fuzzy, it has been more effective to use a word that is specific enough to elicit particular experiences, yet allows for substitution. One woman in my original interviews, who described herself as an atheist, found that she could use the word *God* as a placeholder for a sense of the divine. She found that she reported frequent Daily Spiritual Experiences as measured by the questions, even though she explicitly did not believe in God. For her, these questions pointed to real features of her life.

I often despair when I am trying to use words to communicate my feelings to someone else. I wave my arms around. Sometimes music or visual art captures things better than words. Words fall short of clarity, but we are stuck with them in verbal communication. Chapters 10 and 11 describe how these questions and our answers can help us communicate with those who hold very different beliefs, learning from each other in the process.

In this book I have added alternate wordings after some questions, which you can use as you answer the questions and explore your experiences. Also, half the questions do not include the word *God*, so if nothing works as a substitution, these other items provide opportunity to explore and express your spiritual experiences. My suggestion is that you try to hang loose, stay open, and allow spaciousness as you answer the questions with *God* in them. Notice that these questions do not ask about your abstract beliefs. They are about relationships and experiences. For many people, religious language captures these well. Even those of us who may not be involved in religious community or feel comfortable agreeing with a set of beliefs may still have spiritual experiences, and we need language for these experiences. Over the course of describing your experiences in this book you will continue to unpack your relationship with the divine in your daily life.

The Word *Feel*

In some cultures, including some in the United States, the word *feel* doesn't work as well in describing these experiences, especially with guys. *Sense* is a better word for some people, as in, "I sense God's presence." But for the scientific scale I had to settle on one word or phrase, and the word *feel* worked with people of all educational and social categories in a way that *sense* did not. This scale has been translated into other languages, and the word *feel* works in many cultures. If you want to use the word *sense* rather than *feel* in the individual questions, cross it out and make the substitution. The questions will still work as designed.

Response Categories

The reason for the response categories ("Many times a day," "Every day," "Most days," "Some days," "Once in a while," "Never") is to help you to identify specific moments when you had this feeling or experience and be concrete as you answer the questions. Someone said to me, "These are statements, not questions." But to pick a response category, you need to ask yourself a question. How often do these experiences occur? You need to estimate how often they happen by digging into your memory to identify specific instances. And it is here we find the responses we can describe in words. In some cases, people experienced more of an abiding, constant sense, with peaks and troughs, rather than particular instances. If this was the case, they used the "many times a day" category, and this may work for you as well.

"Never" Is a "Right" Answer

You may never have had some of these experiences. That is just fine. On the other hand, there may be experiences that you have had, but are not aware of. Initially, you may reply "Never," but then as you read about others' experiences in detail, you may think, "I *have* felt something like that." And another possibility is that you might like to have some of these experiences, but just do not have them now. Be honest, and also be willing to be open to feelings like these in the future. Even when you answer, "Never," it may be useful for you to write something about what the absence feels like. You might also find it useful in these situations to write about your feelings in response to one of the quotes or poems.

Why Not Just Answer the Full Set of Questions Straightaway?

You will notice that I do not provide the full set of questions in this book before you have a chance to slowly work through each of them, reflecting on and/or writing about the quality of your particular experiences and reading about a variety of experiences others have had. I have done this on purpose. When the scale is used in research or for assessment purposes, people just answer the full set of multiple-choice questions after reading the introductory statements, and those who administer the scale give them a score on the individual items and a total score. These scores are used in a number of ways. They are used to summarize populations and see if the numbers predict other things. They provide the kinds of research results described in Chapter 5, "Studies Have Shown." They are also used in clinical and organizational settings to see what kinds of resources might be brought to bear to help people. And they are used to look at how people's scores change over time, to see if a particular treatment or program has an effect.

But you are using this scale in a different way in this book. While the numbers may be useful for you, you always have to consider them in the context of the quality of the individual experiences in your days. For this reason, the full scale is in the Appendix, and ways to work with your number scores are not presented until Chapter 4.

Why Write Out Responses to the Questions?

When I read books, I am tempted to just read through exercises that require writing and skip them. Authors tell us to write things down, but that often feels like too much hassle. However, it is worth it to write down responses, either now or later: in a journal, in a dedicated computer file, in your phone or on a tablet, or in some other note-keeping place. Or text or dictate them into your phone and send them to yourself. This book provides some space for you to write notes, but you will probably want to expand on your reflections in another location. Pick something that works for you.

Writing about your experiences can help you become more aware of them. Describing your experiences can help you fix them in your memory. It can allow your mind to grasp them and allow you to mull them over in a different kind of way. However, there may be times when just answering the questions with a numerical response and mentally reflecting are all you feel like doing. In that case, you may decide to return later to do the writing.

Another reason to write about emotional things in life is that it is good for you—physically and mentally. This has been shown in the research of James Pennebaker and others over many years.[4] Briefly writing about stressful and traumatic life events can have long-term positive effects on physical health problems such as asthma and cancer.[5] And writing about positive experiences has also been shown to have good effects.[6]

Your notes can also help you communicate with others (see Chapters 10 and 11). They can provide details for talking with others about things that are important to you in a way they can understand, using the framework of these questions.

Also, your descriptions can inspire others. Your written notes can even inspire *you* in the future during dry patches.

Answering the Questions Again and Again

Answering the questions again and again over time—for example, once a week or once a month—is a good way of bringing the questions and the experiences to mind, and reflecting on the spiritual aspect of your life. It can be useful to track the descriptions of your experiences, your scores on various individual questions, or your total score over time.

Finding Hidden and Not-So-Hidden Treasure in Daily Life

Now let's go through the sixteen questions one by one. You will give yourself a numerical score for each item, and jot down some details of things you "counted" for each. I have also included descriptions of how other people have answered the open-ended questions, and some background to the questions.

The process of answering the questions is something like hunting for hidden Easter eggs or going on a treasure hunt. You may find great chocolate eggs, or those iced eggs with the windows revealing the panorama inside, or ones with the shiny silvery paper and soft insides, or specially flavored jelly beans of some unknown flavor you have never tasted. Other people look in places you never thought of and find treasures of other kinds. Unlike a treasure hunt, however, where the treasures are rare, some of the treasures we find while answering the questions are abundant. Some are out in plain view. What are these treasures? They will be different for each of us, but can include hidden consolation in the midst of sorrow, or moments of peace in the midst of distress, or the satisfaction of giving or receiving love, or awe in nature.

As you go through these questions, you will have a chance to relive things. You may have been rushing through life, too busy to pay much attention at the time. Neuroscience has discovered that memories and images of experiences actually come close to giving us similar benefits to the experience in the moment. Anyone who has daydreamed about lying on the beach or an intimate moment knows this. So hopefully you can enjoy this process of revisiting, and also learn something about yourself, your spirituality, and the flavors of your life.

3 The Daily Spiritual Experience Questions

I was amazed how the rays of lights from the lighthouse revealed some hidden details of the land, how we can rediscover something we have everyday, just in front of us, by a light pointing on it.
—YANN TIERSEN, MUSICIAN

I am spiritually touched by the beauty of creation. ___
Never (1), Once in a while (2), Some days (3),
Most days (4), Every day (5), Many times a day (6)

1

Have you seen pictures from the Hubble telescope? In my college classes I show a photograph of the Horsehead Nebula on the screen. In ungraded journals afterward, many described it as a spiritual experience. A friend of mine, the retired abbot of a monastery and a physicist, views one of these Hubble telescope pictures each morning before prayer, as part of his daily practice. You can check these images out for yourself on the Hubble website.[1] The spiral nebula is one of my favorites. Microscopic images of cells and electron microscope photos of crystalline structures can be amazing, too. But even without these powerful lenses, we can look around us during the day and find things that inspire awe within us.

Here are some examples of experiences of "being spiritually touched by the beauty of creation" from my interviews:

- "I felt this while sitting on the porch during a summer thunderstorm."
- "I saw a tiny baby in the arms of its father and the expression on the father's face."
- "I looked up when I was rock climbing and saw the light bounce off the rock face, and just stopped in my tracks."
- "This happened when I was looking at the top of the clouds out of the airplane window."
- "When I pulled to the side of the road, I sat in the car and watched the sunset on the horizon glow and noticed the colors as they faded."

Experiences of wonder are there for the taking. They are around us every day—awe-inspiring colors and sounds and feelings: signs of and pointers to the transcendent. When we are touched by the beauty of creation, we touch the transcendent as surely as we touch the chairs we sit on. It may seem even more real. When I look out over a lake, watch a sunset from a balcony, see the bud of a flower in a vase in my apartment, watch the flame of a candle, these can give me a vivid sense of the "more than" and a transcendent perspective on my troubles, complaints, and irritations.

What do you see as the beauty of creation? Can you see it in tears? In faces? In the rough and the smooth?

Poetry, through expert use of language, can capture this well and call our attention to these experiences. Seamus Heaney, in his poem "Postscript," inhabits a timeless space between a lake and the ocean on an afternoon's drive on a windy day, and invites us into it:

> . . . You are neither here nor there,
> A hurry through which known and strange things pass

> As big soft buffetings come at the car sideways
> And catch the heart off guard and blow it open.[2]

Visual artists, too, can help us to be more sensitive to the nuances of the natural world, and open us to be spiritually touched by nature in new ways. Someone may photograph something you have seen many times and somehow that photo enables you to see the "more than" more clearly.

If we live in the countryside or near water or spectacular scenery, it can seem easier to be opened up by the transcendent in this way. But even in an urban environment, beauty is there for the taking—in parks, the sky, a baby laughing, light from the window making patterns on the wall, the beauty of people's faces. On the other hand, we may miss the chance to experience this even when it's obvious. When I lived in a village on a mountainside in Switzerland, the Alps were usually in view, but I frequently found myself so consumed by my own preoccupations that I just did not notice this awe-inspiring beauty. These experiences are not defined by the setting, although they may be easier to feel in some places. You may want to find places that particularly help you to see this beauty.

Do you find space in your life for "wow"? There is something about the very substance of life itself that can inspire us, keep our hearts from drying up. When are you aware of it?

As you responded to this question and gave yourself a number score, I expect that you thought about what this meant, in an analytical way. But I hope you thought of specific times, too. Our lives go by so fast: here you get the chance to recapture moments that may have gone by in an instant, and to relive them some in the process.

What are a few experiences that capture this for you? Give yourself a moment to write about some "awesome" times, times when you have felt spiritually touched by the beauty of creation. Pick one that was vivid, and spend some time describing the experience and your feeling about it. Jot down notes of other times—notes that remind you of images. Expand as much as you feel like. You might feel like you could write a whole book! Or you may feel dry. We are individuals. The combination of our life experiences is ours alone, and how each of us experiences this is unique.

Invitation to write . . .

....

....

....

....

....

....

2 **I feel God's presence. ____**
I feel the presence of the divine or holy.[3]
Never (1), Once in a while (2), Some days (3),
Most days (4), Every day (5), Many times a day (6)

Do you ever feel a divine presence or an abiding sense of the holy? How does it feel to you? What does it feel like? Recall it, and get a sense of how your body felt or feels. Is the presence within? Is it personal or impersonal, or both? Is it different at different times?

Connection with the divine or transcendent through a sense of presence is important in both Eastern and Western religious traditions, and it also shapes people's notions of spirituality. The wording of *I feel God's presence*, or *I feel the presence of the divine or holy*, gets at this connection whether we think of it in more theistic terms, a sense of a single divine person, or in less theistic ways. For many, the sense is often hard to capture in words. Giving yourself permission to substitute some other term for *the divine* or *holy*, for the word *God*, may help you to answer this question, especially if the word *God* sends your mind down a cul-de-sac.

Some ways this sense of divine presence was reported were as follows:

- "Sometimes when alone, I feel a comforting presence."
- "When my child was born, I felt God's presence."
- "When I meditate, I feel like I am immersed in a kind of divine ocean."
- A man described being tired and waiting for the bus home, and having the experience of "God's presence, right there, with me, and this happens a lot."
- "I feel a stillness within me."
- A Benedictine monk described this as a physically sensed connection with the "ground of his being."
- A woman who described herself as an atheist said that she felt this occasionally. (She substituted *the divine* for *God*.)

Do we dare to say that we feel the real presence of a being that many say is not real? Perhaps we limit ourselves if we demand that all our sensations fit into limited models of reality. Before we knew that bacteria existed, was an infection any less real? Is God any less real than the table? The table that we see as solid is mostly empty space and energetic bonds, as we now understand molecules. And matter and energy continue to be defined much differently now by physicists than in the days before quantum physics. Great scientists, such as the National Institutes of Health director Francis Collins and many Nobel Prize winners, have been and continue to be very comfortable with the existence of God.[4]

If God does exist, in whatever way we envision the divine, why shouldn't we be able to experience God's presence—the presence of the divine, the holy, the mysterious? Maybe not a taste or a sound, but some kind of sense. What we are aware of is shaped by what we believe is possible. We exclude from awareness that which does not fit our preconceptions.

Throughout the centuries, mystics have described an acute sense of God's presence in many ways. However, this scale is not intended to measure dramatic experiences like hearing God's voice or experiencing ecstatic union. Here we are considering the more ordinary sense of God being with us while doing mundane daily activities, or while doing things like hugging a child or sitting in meditative or prayerful silence.

In *What We Carry*, Dorianne Laux describes in poetry the image of God as a fluttering at the window, and how we are just too tired even to get up and open the window.[5]

Poets and artists describe this feeling better than I can. Visual artists like Rembrandt, Francisco Goya, William Blake, Van Gogh, J. M. W. Turner, and many others communicate this using line, ink, and paint. The poet William Wordsworth, in "Lines Composed a Few Miles above Tintern Abbey," wrote

And I have felt

A presence that disturbs me with the joy

Of elevated thoughts; a sense sublime

Of something far more deeply interfused,

Whose dwelling is the light of setting suns,

And the round ocean, and the living air,

And the blue sky, and in the mind of man,

A motion and a spirit, that impels

All thinking things, all objects of all thought,

And rolls through all things.[6]

Charles Townes, a Nobel Prize–winning physicist, said, "As a religious person, I strongly sense the presence and actions of a creative Being far beyond myself and yet always personal and close by."[7]

Those with a less personal image of God may feel the presence of the divine or the holy in certain places that feel sacred. Does Wordsworth's language speak to this for you? Or the sense of divine presence may feel like it is within you, empowering, strengthening your base from within. You may not have this experience at all. But if you look for it, and find it, what then? Perhaps becoming open to this dimension will bring an increased sense of aliveness to your days. It's not something to be forced, but it is something you might want to remain open to.

Look at the descriptions of experiences of God's presence at the beginning of this section. Have you ever had similar experiences to any of these? Do they remind you of places or times when you have experienced the presence of the divine, the holy, the "more than" in your days? If you have ever had these experiences, spend some time describing what they are like. Remember that, for you, sense or experience might be better words than feel.

Invitation to write . . .

....

....

....

....

....

....

3

I experience a connection to all of life. ____
Never (1), Once in a while (2), Some days (3),
Most days (4), Every day (5), Many times a day (6)

Feeling connected can give me a buzz. Can this be a holy, transcendent feeling? What if this feeling didn't depend on the approval of others, or the groups I belong to, but was more widely available in daily life?

Examples of ways a connection to all of life was experienced, as reported in interviews, included

- "When I am lying on the beach, eyes closed, listening to the waves."
- "When I watch my horse moving so beautifully, I feel something inside myself that feels like grace."
- "When I am part of a group that includes diverse cultures, I feel more connected to the whole world."

- Someone from an indigenous African group reported this when feeling a connection with his ancestors.
- Another person said she had to consciously try to feel this, and she did so by actively drawing attention to her feet on the ground, and thinking of her connection to the earth, the elements, the soil, the rocks, and, through that, to the rest of life.

The "I feel a connection to all of life" question was originally designed to get at that sense of connection that is so important to the spiritual life for Buddhists, Hindus, and those from certain indigenous religions, as well as for agnostics. However, it also ended up resonating with many in other traditions. For example, in the Christian tradition, Francis of Assisi articulated a vision of our links to all creatures and the wider world, writing a song to "brother sun and sister moon." The Native American traditions believe in a Creator, and also maintain a visceral link to all of creation. In addition, people who cannot relate to more established religious structures often find inspiration here. Noticing this connection in daily life might help encourage environmentally sustainable actions, fueling these actions. And rather than seeing life around us as something to battle against, becoming aware that we share life in common with all beings and the wider natural world can promote a more harmonious life.

I got to know a Hindu physician. He helped me see what a good effect recognizing the value in all of life, including my own body, had on me. That connection helped me to feel more grounded, more alive in my own body, rather than feeling like a brain with a body attached for functional purposes. His attitude informed my spirituality, enabling it to become more practical, real, and textured. My body is part of "all of life." It is worth noting here that this is not the same as "zoning out." It is not numbness, but an acute awareness of connection.

I currently am privileged to live in a house where the living room/dining room is surrounded on three sides by windows and natural views. Occasionally, deer race around the house, baby deer sometimes even peek into the windows. It makes me feel part of life—sometimes we are more the "zoo" and the wildlife is looking in on us. Baby deer have grown up in the yard. They look in, recognize us, and go back to munching the plants. For me this encourages a sense of connection. It gives me a more realistic picture of my relationship to life.

In responding to this question, some people report connection to people in the past—more than just a historical connection to others. When standing in the midst of ancient ruins or walking the streets of old cities in Europe, I somehow realize in my gut that the past existed. It is not just a story; it was filled with living, breathing people. In that moment I feel connected to them. And this can lend a spiritual perspective to my present concerns and actions, moving preoccupations of "me" and "mine" out of the center.

This feeling can also provide a link with those who have different religious and cultural beliefs than I do. Although I might feel more connection with those with similar beliefs, I also feel connection with those who have very different beliefs. A sense of common humanity.

Have you ever felt a connection to life that felt spiritual? The natural world, people of many kinds, life in the past? When and where did you feel it? Write some specifics about your experiences. If you find yourself answering "Never" for this question, just pass happily on to the next.

Invitation to write . . .

How close do you feel to God? _____

How close do you feel to the divine or holy?

Not at all close (1), Somewhat close (3), Very close (5),

As close as possible (6)

4

This question doesn't ask you to consider specific moments, but to reflect on how things are for you in general. It gives you a chance to assess an overall feeling in your life. That's why it is scored differently. This complicates the statistics. But feedback from those answering the questions and using the scale over time made me keep it in. A Brazilian researcher thought it was one of the most important questions for the people she worked with, even though it caused an extra complication in her very sophisticated statistical analyses, and she strongly argued for continuing to include it.

Some people envision the divine within them. For others, God is far away and inaccessible. Still others experience an interpersonal closeness. For many, various images meld. And these feelings can ebb and flow in daily life. To answer the question, pick your average experience.

I was in Greece for some meetings on the nature of the human person. One thing that I found fascinating was learning some Greek words. (Pronouncing them was another story—just saying *thank you* required major reorganization of my mouth!) The Greeks do a great job describing philosophical and theological concepts. There is a Greek word *hypostasis*, ὑπόστᾰσις. It does not have an exact equivalent in English. The closest might be "ground of being," but that does not fully capture its meaning. It describes a foundational element of the human person that is linked to the divine. Christians, in the concept of the Trinity, a three-in-one vision of God, talk about the Holy Spirit, that aspect of God that is present within the individual person. But this does not clearly reflect this notion of *hypostasis*. Our theologies, our religious texts, our philosophical descriptions, approximate reality. Words ultimately let us down, but that does not keep us from continuing to try. Words provide the main way to share our experiences with others. This word helps me to consider what closeness to God might be like.

Religions differ on how or even if divine closeness exists. Some envision a divine being who is distant, but most major religions have some way in which a divine being, who is seen as Creator, can also be seen as close. Nearness in time, nearness in space—or maybe just "nearness," not further defined. However experienced, this sense of closeness can be a very uplifting spiritual experience in our daily lives, changing the way we experience who we are and our relationships with others.

In response to this item, one of the Cistercian monks I interviewed said, "This is primary for a monk, it is *the* question for a monk." The monks particularly resonated with this item. Two monks stated that closeness was not a matter of feeling but of will. One of the monks said, "The more we go to the presence of God in contemplation ... the more of God we see in daily life." Another said, "God has no grandchildren. . . . We are all children . . . close and direct."

In a radio interview, Rabbi Harold Kushner, author of *When Bad Things Happen to Good People*, mentioned asking a group of Jewish middle-school students how many believed in God, and he received silence.[8] But later in the discussion, he asked how many had felt close to God, and many answered positively. This DSES question does not ask about belief, but creates space for you to examine your experience of the divine in a more direct way.

Remember, there are no "right" answers. Some of us just do not feel close to God, or close to the divine in any way. For some this is just fine. But for others it may carry with it an experience of alienation. Guilt, too, can make me feel distant from God. Certain religious traditions, such as Judaism and Christianity, have liturgy and specific practices that help to resolve a perception of distance caused by guilt. Religious language using the more familiar forms of *you* (e.g., *du* in German and *tu* in French) encourages a sense of interpersonal intimacy. Liturgical practices of washing, fasting, and repentance are often designed to resolve this sense of distance, enabling us to feel closer to the divine. Practices such as silence and meditative prayer can help some move from feelings of alienation to a solitude that connects with the "ground of being."

What does closeness to God feel like to you? Do you ever feel so close to the divine that you experience no sense of separation, or is it more like personal closeness where you remain somewhat distinct?

Invitation to write . . .

....

....

....

....

....

....

....

5

**I desire to be closer to God or in union
with the divine.** ____
Never (1), Once in a while (2), Some days (3),
Most days (4), Every day (5), Many times a day (6)

Intimacy. What is it, and do I want it? We have relationships with other people in our lives: family, friends, lovers. Some of us find intimacy easily in these settings; some not so much. When we are in a close romantic relationship with someone, we can have moments when we feel like we blend with the other. Sometimes just being quiet together with a friend can feel so good. We desire to be close to those we like and trust.

This question speaks to a wide variety of experiences. Maybe you feel so close to the divine that you have no desire to be closer. Or maybe you do not desire intimacy with the divine at all—it seems too hot to handle! Maybe you desire to experience closeness to a transcendent being—God in the widest sense of the word—but cannot imagine that it's possible.

Some of the moments people described in response to this question illustrate this complexity:

- "Sometimes I feel very alienated and life feels meaningless, and at some of these times I long for closeness to a divine source."
- "I don't believe in God, but I somehow long to be closer to something greater than myself—God experienced in a new way."
- "It feels like God desires to be close to me, but I keep God at a distance. I don't want to be close."
- "This feeling I get while sitting on the beach with someone I am close to—the sounds and the feeling just take over and I am no longer anxious. I feel more connected to the person next to me, and also to something more than that, and I lose self-conscious feelings. I want more of that in my life."
- "God is love, and I want to be as close to that all-encompassing love as possible."

This item was added during the course of the interviews, when I asked people what I might be leaving out. I heard from them about a longing for an interaction with or relationship to the divine, especially when that sense of closeness was not there. This point was raised originally by agnostics, but has ended up also being important for people immersed in a faith tradition.

Stevie Smith, the English poet, wrote,

> There is a God in whom I do not believe
> Yet to this God my love stretches.[9]

The theme of longing for closeness recurs in popular music in ways that often stretch beyond romantic attachments. When I first heard Supertramp's song "Even in the Quietest Moments," I found myself applying the words to longing for the divine. Yusuf Islam (Cat Stevens) includes this sentiment in his most recent music from a Muslim perspective. Joe Pugh does this in a very American way.[10] Great gospel songs and other religious music also do this. You could probably identify lines from favorite songs that suit your tastes or era. The combination of lyrics with musical cadences powerfully evokes these feelings of transcendent longing. When we listen for this, we hear it more often.

This desire was important to the physicist Isidor Isaac Rabi, who won a Nobel Prize in 1944. He wrote,

> Physics filled me with awe, put me in touch with a sense of original causes. Physics brought me closer to God. That feeling stayed with me throughout my years in science. Whenever one of my students came to me with a scientific project, I asked only one question, "Will it bring you nearer to God?"[11]

The great religious love poetry of the Hebrews—for example, in the Song of Songs or the Psalms—contains vivid imagery of desire and longing.

Our desires are central to our daily lives. Other human beings ultimately fall short of truly satisfying our desires. And not all relationships are good for us. In a book I coedited on social support research and practice,[12] we emphasized that close relationships with other people are not always good. We certainly don't need another negative relationship! We want a relationship with the transcendent that is a healthy one. The desire for closeness to the transcendent implies a relationship that will be a positive force in our lives.

I have come to know Muslims from Turkey and Egypt, and found that desire for God is central to their lived faith. It is connected with their love of God. The poetry of Rumi, a thirteenth-century Muslim poet from the Sufi tradition, has had a recent revival.[13] The appeal of his poetry stretches beyond his tradition. His poetry captures a passionate longing for God, and the "transcendent real" that is grounded in our bodies and the natural world:

> There is some kiss we want with
> our whole lives, the touch of
> spirit on the body. Seawater
> begs the pearl to break its shell.[14]

Do you desire to be closer to the "fountain of all holiness"? Do you feel alienated? Do you feel a longing to be closer to God? Describe these feelings.

Invitation to write . . .

....

....

....

....

....

....

6

I feel God's love for me directly. ___
I feel divine love for me directly.
Never (1), Once in a while (2), Some days (3),
Most days (4), Every day (5), Many times a day (6)

Love from a divine source—what a powerfully uplifting experience that can be. Even if we believe "God loves me" in the abstract, that does not mean we feel God's love directly very often. Even very religious people can long for this and just not find it. In interviews, they often admit that this feeling is elusive in daily life.

Some people have not been in situations where others express compassionate love to them. This is sad. To experience love from others, it has to be expressed in the first place! However, even in these life situations, many report that an ever-present divine love is there to draw on, to fill the tank.

Here are a few examples from the interviews:

- "When I feel like I have screwed up and I sense God's forgiveness, that God is OK with me."
- "Looking at an icon of Mary with the child Jesus, the love I see expressed there penetrates to my core."
- "When I feel abandoned by others, mistreated by others, I feel God's acceptance and welcome."
- "During religious liturgy." (This was mentioned by those in a variety of traditions.)
- "In the midst of loving-kindness meditation." (Buddhists and others expressed this.)
- "When reciting the Jesus prayer" (Lord have mercy, *Kyrie Eleison*).
- "When I think back on happy events, I have a sense of being cared for."

- "When I rest in God's love for me, I feel like a child in its mother's arms."

Religious traditions articulate a relationship with a divine being in various ways, and most theologies would say that people can experience divine love directly. The reality of the love that God feels for us is often beautifully expressed in the poetic language of religious writings and scriptures. In the Song of Songs, for example, God is quoted speaking to us:

> Arise, come, my darling; my beautiful one, come with me.
> My dove in the clefts of the rock, in the hiding places on
> the mountainside, show me your face, let me hear your
> voice; for your voice is sweet, and your face is lovely.[15]

On the other hand it is worth recalling that Mother Teresa had long periods in her life when she did not feel this direct love. So if your answer to this question is "once in a while" or even "never," you are in good company!

There are many obstacles to receiving love. If I think I am undeserving of love, that is a big obstacle—I just don't let love in.

And there are other barriers to love. A friend gave me a great Valentine's Day card. It was a cartoon of a man in a dark apartment, with all sorts of locks and barricades on the inside of his apartment door.[16] He was standing inside, looking down at the floor under the door. And there scooting under the door was a tiny card with a little pink heart on it. I saw myself in that man. I close the door, barricade myself in. I don't want to be vulnerable. No wonder I don't feel God's love.

Divine love is framed up in many religious traditions as a love that overcomes our shortcomings, our weaknesses, our failings. Divine love that is unconditional. In a Christian model I am familiar with, God's love is always there; we just have to "tune in." Reflecting on the good things in your life, and seeing many of them as undeserved gifts, can also uncover this feeling.

Love from others can fall short of our desire for unconditional love. We fail one another continually, even with the best of motives. This is where divine love can fill a space in our hearts, and does so for many. Rabindranath Tagore, the Bengali Nobel prizewinner, wrote:

> By all means they try to hold me secure who love me in this world. But it is otherwise with thy love, which is greater than theirs, and thou keepest me free. Lest I forget them they never venture to leave me alone. But day passes by after day and thou are not seen. If I call not thee in my prayers, if I keep not thee in my heart—thy love for me still waits for my love.[17]

In my living room I have a Greek Orthodox icon of the Mother and Child I purchased in Athens. When I look at it, and allow it to work on me, the love in the image somehow penetrates me. Not just an intellectual understanding that God cares for me, but a visceral sense of divine reality that pulls me in and comforts me.

The word *feel* is in this item. You could try changing the wording to *experience* or *sense*, and see how you might answer it—whether that allows you to connect better with your own experience of divine love. *Feel* might just be too much of a physical word for you. Try out these other options or ones of your own, and try to find one that gets at this kind of experience for you.

Write down what it has felt like for you if you have experienced this. Think about the circumstances in detail and write about them. These notes can be a storehouse for you to draw on in the future and to share with others.

Invitation to write . . .

....

....

....

....

....

....

I feel God's love for me through others. _____
I feel divine love for me through others.
Never (1), Once in a while (2), Some days (3),
Most days (4), Every day (5), Many times a day (6)

7

There is something powerful about being loved when nothing is expected in return. When I am appreciated and valued, not for what I can do, but for the person I am, with my flaws and weaknesses as well as my strengths. When others really want me to flourish. There is a kind of purity of heart about this kind of love, like the love in the frequently cited Corinthians passage, "Love is patient, love is kind . . ."[18]—which is surely poetry. There seems to be a transcendent power here. *Love* is such a misused word in the English language, with so many meanings. That's why *God's love, divine love,* is used in this item. This scale is looking at spiritual experiences, experiences of the "more than" in our lives. For many of us, this comes through the care and love we receive from family, friends, and sometimes even strangers.

Some examples of the shape this experience can take as reported by others:

- "A kind smile from a stranger in a public place."
- "The touch of a hand and eye contact during the sign of peace at church."
- "Cooked dinner with a warm smile from my spouse."
- "A backrub."
- "Encouraging words in the workplace."
- "A hug in response to my apology."
- "My mother's love for me."
- "When imaginatively remembering a time when I was really loved by someone in a solid way without expectations."
- "While hearing Mr. Rogers say, 'I like you just the way you are.'"
- "While wearing a hand-knitted scarf from my sister."

During the interviews, many resonated with this question. Those who did not believe in a god were still comfortable reporting this experience. When asked if they had a problem with it being called *God's love,* many agnostics and atheists said they used the translation instructions from the introduction and felt that this kind of love was different, special. For some, divine love, compassionate love, most often comes from those close to us.

Some of us have difficulty trusting others, so we don't experience this kind of love from others very often. Or we may not have been put in situations where this kind of love has been there for us. Or, when it is there for us, we discount it, or disregard it, due to past experiences of being let down by others. We find that the "direct line" of love from the divine is the more frequent source of love for us. Even if this is true for you, I hope you can find some of these events in your life to jot down here.

Receiving love is important. That seems so obvious—surely that should be easy and we should be focusing on giving love. But we often find it hard to receive love. We give love to others to enable them to flourish, for them to benefit somehow from our love. So when others love you, they, too, want you to benefit or flourish. Can we graciously receive love with an attitude of appreciation that does not disparage the care others express? Can we rest in the glorious feeling of it, like a warm bath?

It surprised me that a few of the Christian monks said in the interviews that this was the only way they felt God's love. They live such an explicitly religious life, with frequent scriptural assurance of the love of God. But perhaps, given their close sense of community and the value placed on divine love in the monastery, they experienced more expression of selfless caring and had more acute perception of it in the midst of their days. When one of the monks said that it was easier to feel God's love through others than directly, he identified this as "support and acceptance." Some other comments from the monks included, "Through others—this is the obvious way to experience the spiritual . . . receiving love from them" and "God can act through people, loving providence."

For many of us, this is the main source of love in our lives. It depends on there being people willing to express other-centered love to us. But another thing is critical. We need to be attentive, and listen for it.

Do you find divine love in your relationships with other people? Describe where and when you have felt this kind of love.

Invitation to write . . .

....

....

....

....

....

....

8 **I feel a selfless caring for others.** _____
Never (1), Once in a while (2), Some days (3),
Most days (4), Every day (5), Many times a day (6)

Giving love can give you a buzz. Seeing someone else's face light up, or feeling you have contributed to their success. Lifting someone else's spirits with a kind word. Even praying for someone else. Desiring that things will turn out well for them, and putting the enthusiasm of your hopes behind that in prayer, can take you out of your own immediate concerns, and be liberating and satisfying. Although it helps to see the joy in the person receiving your gift or care, just the feeling of selfless caring has the capacity to enliven you.

The last two questions were about love coming into you, you

being the object of love—"love in." In this question and the next you will be considering how you feel love for others—"love out." Since the DSES measures your experiences rather than your actions, you will draw your attention to attitudes toward others that might promote other-centered love. In the last question you thought about how it feels to receive love. When we receive this kind of accepting, freely given love, it is great. And in your jottings you described how it felt to receive this kind of love from other people. Even if you did not write anything down, you remembered. I expect that the attitude of the giver was important to what you felt.

Now, how do you give love to others? Giving without necessarily expecting a payback is also a spiritual experience. Consider the feeling of giving love—your inner attitude—when you are giving freely, not just because you "have to." Love centered on the good of the other person. How does this feel for you?

Here are some examples of times when people felt this:

- "When working in a soup kitchen for homeless people."
- "Getting up in the night to care for my baby when she is crying and I am tired."
- "I am a nurse and when I care for patients I often give more of myself than is required."
- "Desiring that someone else succeed in a work setting in a way that might jeopardize my standing."
- "Allowing someone who looks harassed to step in front of me in line."
- "Buying groceries for a sick neighbor."
- "When I help out someone I don't like."
- "Giving to a charity online."

This item, *I feel a selfless caring for others*, was designed to reach all kinds of people. Its words needed to be straightforward and easily understood. And it has had to hold up to translations into many languages. In the interviews, I explicitly asked if the wording meant you had to be totally selfless—I hoped not, as that was not the intention. I experimented with a variety of wordings, and ultimately settled on this one. For most people, it indicated attitudes that were centered on the good of the other rather than oneself. I excluded wording that indicated a kind of martyrdom, a "poor me" attitude. This item is not about abnegation of self, denying all our own interests.

All our care and love for others has mixed motivation. There seems to be some self-centered motivation present in even our most selfless behaviors. So do not be too scrupulous when you answer this question. Is the attitude you have, the feeling you have, centered on the good of the other person? Or is the central motivation your own benefit? We can be fundamentally other-centered, have a selfless caring for others, even when we find joy in the process. (We will be discussing this in more detail in Chapter 6, "The Flow of Love.")

"Selfless caring for others" is different when directed toward those you are close to than toward strangers. Sometimes it can even be easier to feel this toward strangers, given the irritations and lack of self-awareness that often occur in close relationships.

Jot down some specific times you have felt this other-centered love. Do you have this feeling toward strangers? Do you have it toward those you are close to? Also describe how it feels to you. Does it bring you pleasure? Does it weigh you down? Or both?

Invitation to write . . .

....

....

....

....

....

I accept others even when they do things I think are wrong. ____
Never (1), Once in a while (2), Some days (3),
Most days (4), Every day (5), Many times a day (6)

9

The quality of mercy is not strain'd,
It droppeth as the gentle rain from heaven
Upon the place beneath. It is twice blest:
It blesseth him that gives and him that takes.
—WILLIAM SHAKESPEARE[19]

This question is one of my personal favorites because it highlights an undervalued spiritual experience. When we think about receiving love from others, or directly from a divine source, one of the most wonderful features of the feeling is its unconditional nature. No matter whether we have behaved well or not, we are loved—loved through thick and thin. This is the kind of love we give to others when we fundamentally accept people even when we disagree with them, or even when they are doing things we think are wrong. This is not to say that the wrong is not wrong.

We do not necessarily excuse the wrong done. But we see their value as deeper than their actions. Forgiveness is something that is focused on the event and is complicated. But mercy is an attitude of heart, a fundamental acceptance of others. And it is a potentially liberating spiritual experience that can feed us as it flows out into the world around us.

Here are some examples of times when others feel this in their lives:

- "When I genuinely smile at a stranger."
- "When disciplining my teenage son, while sending messages about my basically positive attitude to him."
- "When expressing kindness to someone in my office who irritates me."
- "When I just 'let it go.'"
- "I cut people slack in daily situations. Who knows what circumstances they are dealing with?"
- "When considering someone to be part of my community, even though he or she has different beliefs than I do."

Recent research on newlyweds examined what predicted a good relationship years later.[20] The study included the sixteen questions you have been answering. The combination of acute awareness of faults of the loved one, combined with thinking them wonderful, predicted a healthy relationship years later. Lack of awareness of the failings of the husband or wife predicted a less healthy relationship years later, and one more likely to end in divorce. Often we think that to love people, feel close to them, we need to ignore their failings and weaknesses. But accepting them even while noticing faults—that lets true love flourish.

The underlying attitude that this question tries to address is that of mercy and acceptance. Mercy is not pitying people, but rather seeing intrinsic value in them. This can include giving someone the benefit of the doubt, or dealing with others' faults in light of one's own. Mercy, as presented in this item, is closely linked to forgiveness, yet is a deeper experience than isolated acts of forgiveness. This question asks about a felt sense of mercy. This is different than just thinking that mercy is a good quality to have.

This item is the last in the group of questions that specifically captures the "flow of love" in our lives. In some ways it can also describe moments of self-acceptance. Can I extend to myself the graciousness that I feel for others? Can I take on the "scientific" attitude to myself, thinking of myself as "another"? And then do I accept myself, even when I do things I think are wrong? Your attitude toward others and your attitude toward yourself feed off each other. If I have trouble accepting others, how does that affect my attitude toward myself? Do I deny my own failings in order to accept myself? Or do I just face them head-on, and see my value nonetheless?

In the structured interviews I did on compassionate love,[21] one monk said, "We are all foolish and stupid in so many ways, and it is so important to accept people anyway." Another said, "My awareness of my own failings really helps me have this experience. . . . Self-knowledge helps me not to judge others."

Recognizing behavior that is wrong provides us with the opportunity for the spiritual experience of mercy, acceptance. Do you think everything is right, that everyone behaves in ways that are right? Most of us, even though we try to be politically correct, think some things are wrong, and that some people behave badly. Can we hate the action, but accept the person? In some ways mercy takes work, it goes against the grain. But on the other hand, it can be a freeing and liberating spiritual experience.

What are some of the times you have accepted others even when they have done things you think are wrong? Jot down one or two specific instances and note what it felt like. This could be with strangers or with people you are close to. Did it affect your relationship with the person? And what about accepting yourself? Do you treat yourself with mercy? Do you value yourself while also accurately seeing areas where you fall short, or when doing things you would rather not have done?

Invitation to write . . .

....

....

....

....

....

....

10

I find strength in my religion or spirituality. _____
Never (1), Once in a while (2), Some days (3),
Most days (4), Every day (5), Many times a day (6)

In a recent e-mail updating a friend, my writing sounded like a passage from a novel: "When we last heard from our heroine . . ." When I think of a hero, it is not someone like me. But what is courage anyway? Tough times hit all of us, to varying degrees.

Tough times can be brought on by events beyond our control or as we struggle with inner demons of anxiety and fear, when things wouldn't be described by others as being all that bad.

In difficult times I often just tell myself to buck up. This lasts for short periods, but it doesn't keep me going over the long haul. Ultimately, what has most sustained me, gotten me over the hurdles—when I was a single mom with three daughters and a chronic illness, or struggling with a difficult job—has been a reliance on strength beyond myself, within myself: eternal presence. What gets us through the tough times—you and me?

A young mother from inner-city Chicago talked to me about coming home after an exhausting day of work, and still being able to look after her children, finding strength from beyond herself. A middle-aged man mentioned that strength from his religion helped him to confront his boss on an ethical issue, despite fear of losing his job. An urban adolescent girl said, "I am able to have courage to do some things because I know God has my back." A recovering alcoholic said that strength from God helped him to resist the urge to drink alcohol again.

Other descriptions of this sense of strength from those interviewed included

- "I have confidence in a power greater than I am, to help get me through."
- "I have a feeling in my gut that I can make it."
- "I feel support from my religious community."
- "God will help us endure any stress. I have power in my heart."
- "I think of those who have lived courageous spiritual lives and it gives me courage to keep going." Examples given were Dag Hammarskjöld, Mahatma Gandhi, Mother

Teresa, Jesus, Moses, Muhammad, Siddhartha Gautama (Buddha), and Martin Luther King Jr.

This question has *religion or spirituality* in it. For many, the spiritual in daily life includes a set of religious beliefs and the community of people living out those beliefs together. This can give a structural integrity to life, like the intertwined fibers of a rope. However, we can have this spiritual experience both within the context of organized religion and outside of it. For some, the organized religious structure can actually be undermining. Beyond the strength that belonging and beliefs may give, many religious and nonreligious people feel internal support in a direct way from a divine power, higher power, or power that fuels from within.

Leontyne Price, the opera singer, talked about praying before going on stage: "I wouldn't be here if You didn't arrange it, and I really need You to get me through the next four acts."

Rainer Maria Rilke, a Czech-German poet writing in the late 1800s and early 1900s, took an eclectic approach; he was not traditionally religious at all. In this poem, he describes God walking out into the world with each of us, encouraging us to feel the strength of our feelings and explore our yearnings; and in the midst of it all offering us companionship.

God speaks to each person
before creating us,
then accompanies each of us silently out of the night.
These are the clouded words we hear:

Sent out by your senses,
go to the full extent of your yearning. . . .

Let everything happen: beauty and terror.
No feeling is ultimate.
You must just keep going:
Do not separate yourself from me.

The land they call Life
is near.

You'll recognize it
by its seriousness.
Give me your hand.[22]

Do you ever feel the presence of God as companionship in the midst of your traumas and adventure?

You have particular things that you find hard. Where do you go for extra oomph? When involved in research on stress, I was particularly interested in what causes resilience. Why do some people fold in difficult circumstances or burn out over time, while others are able to keep going? For example, it takes strength to face an addiction and do something about it. Addictions of various kinds can keep us reacting and running. Alcoholics Anonymous has helped many with alcohol abuse. Built into its twelve steps is the need to rely on a "higher power" in order to handle the pull of an addiction. Although not as dramatic as being an alcoholic, we all may be "driven" to do things in ways similar to addiction to drugs. Examples of this include playing video games, checking social websites in excess, spending too much time shopping online or surfing the Web, or obsessively worrying. Have you ever found yourself doing things repeatedly that get in the way of doing things you value, feeling driven rather than freely choosing? Where do you find the strength to control this? Do you ever rely on strength from a source "more than" yourself in these circumstances?

Sometimes the difficulties facing you are beyond your control, such as illness or the behaviors of others. Are you experiencing some of those now? Where do you find that extra oomph to resist addictive behaviors or to get you through difficult times?

What are some of your sources of strength? Are there times when you have found this kind of strength from your spirituality or religiousness, and if so, how did it work for you? Be specific about your feelings. Did it affect your life or that of others? If so, how?

Invitation to write . . .

....

....

....

....

11 **I find comfort in my religion or spirituality. ____**
Never (1), Once in a while (2), Some days (3),
Most days (4), Every day (5), Many times a day (6)

Comfort is such a lovely feeling. What do you find comfort in? Eating good food? A caring hug? Reassuring words from a friend? I lived in Belfast, Northern Ireland, for ten years. At that time central heating was not a staple, and I spent much of my time there cold and damp and wheezing, breathing in the sulfur fumes of coal fires, a stranger in that city wracked by violence and mistrust. I longed to be warm and dry. I longed to be somewhere I belonged. Don't we all want to be comfortable? And my situation was minor compared to the major discomforts many face.

As I write this today, my situation is relatively cozy. But I still manage to feel uneasy in this good situation. Small sorrows, sadnesses, or insecurities can plague us even in the best of times. The kind of comfort that can be provided by religion or spirituality is independent of the situation. We look to be soothed by eating and drinking, by buying things, by finding distractions. But there is a source of soothing that can be found in a spiritual perspective that is there no matter what the circumstances. Comfort is linked to a sense of our bodies. Comfort from spiritual or religious sources can comfort deeply, within yet beyond the context of our bodies.

Examples of specific times in other people's lives when they found comfort in their religion or spirituality include

- "After losing my job, my spiritual beliefs helped to put things in perspective."
- "When a member of my religious community comforts me."
- "After my child died, religious liturgy was a comfort to me."
- "Reading spiritual writings can ease me when I am anxious."
- "It gives me comfort to know I can call upon Allah."
- "When I feel alienated, my spirituality gives me a sense of belonging to something that is not ephemeral."
- "Christ suffered, and it is comforting to know that he went through hard times and understands."

Do we take advantage of this source of comfort as much as we could? Awareness of the big picture, the transcendent, can put physical and psychological pain in perspective. Looking to a divine source for comfort can be cultivated as a habit. When we think of the many things we look to for comfort, most can disappear. The transcendent, God, the divine, as described in many religious and spiritual traditions, is always there, even when we might not be aware of that presence.

Unfortunately, this spiritual experience tends to be more frequent in tough times. However, that is when we need it most. Someone suffering from cancer of the bone marrow said,

> Apart from God, I find no meaning able to bear a life's weight. This proposition is both ontological and mystical. Nothing in my experience makes a center that holds. . . . Without a God who works in my experience but also escapes it and transcends it . . . the grass withers. The flowers fade. All of our bones dry up and fracture sooner or later. The only bedrock I have found for rest is the stunning fact (unavoidable empirical reality) that there is always more—outside of me, within me, for my body, for my mind, historically, socially.[23]

When things make sense, fit together, we feel more comfortable. Research has shown that when faced with the possibility of death, we try our best to manage the terror of that, and we do this through various psychological strategies. We make real efforts to suppress thoughts and behaviors that seem to contradict one another.[24] We do our best to find meaning in life, and that provides comfort in and of itself. It seems to be part of the way we are. Religious and spiritual writings, theological systems that have been worked out in practice over centuries, can provide a framework that helps make sense of a rather troubling world by addressing things below the surface, by including the transcendent real in the equation. The Twenty-Third Psalm has been a comfort for many over the centuries. Set to music or recited from memory, it does not minimize hardships in its language but it contains concrete images of transcendent comfort. *In green pastures, beside still waters, my soul restored . . . surely goodness and mercy will follow me all the days of my life.* I remember one time drawing pictures for each image in this psalm, to help me memorize it, and it allowed the comfort to work its way into me, and pop up unexpectedly during the day.

Julian of Norwich, a fourteenth-century hermit in Great Britain, is quoted often: "All will be well, and all will be well, and all manner of thing will be well."[25] Things will, of course, go wrong in life at various levels, but nevertheless this statement speaks beyond that.

Do you ever find a spiritual source of comfort in your daily life? Where and when? What did it feel like? Jot down some specifics from your life. If you have never experienced this, take time to just write about some tough times and how you felt.

Invitation to write . . .

12

I feel guided by God in the midst of daily activities. _____
I feel divine guidance in the midst of daily activities.
Never (1), Once in a while (2), Some days (3),
Most days (4), Every day (5), Many times a day (6)

We use our wits to maneuver through daily life. Some of our decision making is on the surface—we know our reasons and act accordingly. Sometimes, however, we make decisions with our gut—we act spontaneously, intuitively, not exactly knowing why. Often we cannot identify what is "driving the bus" of our decisions. If we knew everything about the situation and ourselves and could predict the future perfectly, we could make a perfect decision. But this is never the case. There are always unknown variables influencing our choices, and we cannot completely predict the future, no matter how much we try.

Some responses to this question include

- "When I am wondering what to do, I can feel God nudging me in a certain direction."
- "I get a flash of inspiration that seems to come from a transcendent source."
- "I work together with God to solve problems."
- "In the voice of my conscience, I sense advice from a greater wisdom than myself."
- "I sense God's caution sometimes, and encouragement at other times."

A Greek Orthodox saying is, "Put your mind in your heart as you go through the day."[26] I find this a very helpful image. Divine guidance can operate from within us, when we put our mind in our heart—the heart, the core of our being.

If God is all-seeing but we still have free will, that is an apparent paradox. But many things that look like paradoxes reveal underlying coherence, and end up making more sense than dissecting things into their parts and trying to jam them back into a cohesive whole. I have fallen in love with the poems of certain poets because they present a paradox that nonetheless leaves space for coherence. I can hear a divine voice in certain poetry and music lyrics if I listen deeply and let them work on me. The Chinese poetry of Chuang Tzu is an example of this for me—it challenges my linear approach to problem solving.[27]

A wise friend of mine once told me, "Don't push the river." Can we relax, floating on the surface, and then sometimes use the breaststroke to avoid obstacles or swim to shore for a rest? Can we look for and see underlying divine guidance that is available? Do we take advantage of this? This does not mean totally relaxing and drowning. Rather, it means having realistic ideas of our actual ability to control events and the role of other circumstances beyond our control, and gracefully fitting in where we can make the most of things.

Jane, a dear friend, signed up for tango lessons in her sixties. Dance, she says, teaches us about life, especially a life of faith. She shared some of the things she learned with me, including that God, the divine, leads, and we follow—but in the way of a dance, not like leading an animal by the nose. Our movement is in response to the music. There are set steps and patterns, but we also have the capacity to improvise. The relationship with the other person is key in dancing with a partner—you must trust your partner and know your partner's subtleties. This relationship grows over time. There is liveliness in it all—the tango is not boring!

Dancing is graceful. *Grace* means gift, power, and strength flowing in and through.

Since we usually do not see the long-term implications of our actions—what is really going to be lasting and change our lives and those of others—we need to listen to the deeper music and pay attention to it. We are here, on the spot, doing our best. We act in the moment without being able to see the future. If there is a "more than," then being in harmony with that has the capacity to make our actions more effective in areas of real importance.

How do we tell if the guidance is from a divine source? Not easy and clear-cut for sure, and the issue is one that various religions have struggled with over the centuries, trying to establish guidelines. The issue is discernment—is this the right thing for me to do now? One of the monks I interviewed said, "When my response to a situation that is beyond my capabilities is a creative one . . . pieces come together." Another mentioned the essential relationship of commandments and conscience. One person I interviewed described how morning prayer prepared him to expect God's actions and help throughout the day, opening his capacity to be aware of them. These responses describe a sense of reassurance, a feeling that the choice "feels right," and an engagement of the gut in the analysis.

Martin Smith, an Episcopalian monk, in a presentation on prayer, said that God is continually calling on the phone. It is ringing, but we are just not picking up. Are we so busy doing other things, and wanting things to go a certain way, that we just do not listen?

Even after working with this list of questions for over fifteen years, I find that going back to the specifics of the items, writing down my experiences, helps me to spot them. This challenges me to think specifically about just how this might work in my life today—and how they might work in my life has changed over the years. I can only crudely describe how divine guidance operates in my daily life, but metaphors of various kinds can help me nevertheless.

What helps you make decisions? How are you reassured that your decision is right? Describe any times when you tap into a greater wisdom as you make decisions in your life. In the midst of daily life, do you find yourself engaging with divine guidance? How does this feel? Does it help?

Invitation to write . . .

....

....

....

....

....

....

I ask for God's help in the midst of daily activities. ____
I ask for help from a higher power in the midst of daily activities.
Never (1), Once in a while (2), Some days (3),
Most days (4), Every day (5), Many times a day (6)

13

"God help me!" Somehow this exclamation, expressed silently or aloud, does not depend on our belief system. Many who say they don't believe in God will pray when a plane they are on is in trouble or in other desperate circumstances. Have you ever asked for God's help when things looked particularly bleak? For example, when you were faced with a car coming straight at you in traffic or when you heard bad news on the health front. We may not have a clear conception of who God is or what God is like, but in crises we still can find ourselves asking for God's help or help from a higher power.

Whether and how we get a response is not within the scope of this book. In this question I am focusing more on when and how the asking for help happens, and how this is a spiritual experience that can enhance life. We are asking without judging, and reflecting on how this is experienced by many people in many ways.

A major tenet of the widespread twelve-step Alcoholics Anonymous program for addictions—addictions to things as disparate as substances and gambling—is that I alone am not enough. I need help—from others, from a higher power. This forms part of the twelve steps, which appeal to people from religious and nonreligious backgrounds alike. And it runs counter to a cultural model of total self-reliance as the ideal way to be. So are we admitting weakness if we ask for God's help? And is that terrible?

In reality, we all need help at times. We needed help as children, and most of us will need help as we age. So is total self-sufficiency an illusion? Seeking help from a higher power, asking for divine help, is often an appropriate response.

How this actually might work out is not at all clear. Does God or a higher power answer prayers through changing circumstances? Or is there some other way that the divine becomes active once we open ourselves to a transcendent power beyond ourselves that seeks good for us and for others around us? Answers to prayer aren't always easy to figure. The answer might not be what we asked for. Something about the seeking of grace, seeking input, seeking help may in itself change circumstances and how we fit into the flow of things.

This question about asking for divine help does not assume that you expect God to intervene with a lightning bolt. I personally do not think of myself as a person having great faith. But I do ask for help. There is something about just living with a willingness to ask for help that somehow adds to my life. I don't know what the answer will look like. But I expect that somehow it is heard, that it can be part of a dialogue with a caring and active ultimate reality interested in my well-being and that of all other people.

Some specific times people mentioned asking for divine assistance include

- "When I'm uncertain, I turn to a higher power for advice."
- "I find myself exclaiming silently, 'Help me.'"
- "When I want to do something that I know is not good for me and want to resist the urge."
- "When dealing with my parents, and wanting more patience than I have."
- "Prayer gives me mental help."
- "It gives me comfort to know I can call upon Allah to guide me. I know I can ask for help from Allah."
- "I am in chronic pain and ask for God's help to do basic things."

This question identifies times when we "go to God for social support," as an agnostic scientist at the National Institute on Aging summed it up. Some of the people interviewed who responded to this item with "Some days" or "Once in a while" do not necessarily report believing that help will be forthcoming, but asking for God's help was a positive experience nevertheless. As we will see later, in looking at the data collected on this question, people with a variety of beliefs report some experience of asking for help. This item represents something that is understood and acknowledged to occur by a wide range of the general population.

John Cassian, a writer from the first century who helped shape the Benedictine spiritual tradition, suggested that throughout the day one should repeatedly use the phrase "O God, come to my assistance/O Lord, make haste to help me," to cultivate connection to the divine.[28] A Hispanic woman saw the incorporation of this kind of prayer as something ordinary, like the other practical things of daily life. God is not a magician, but somehow works within the order of the world. But what that order is and how it functions, we only know in part.

Asking for help can also be seen as lowering the barriers to divine input. C. S. Lewis wrote something that made a huge difference to me in the way I lived my life. It continues to challenge me personally:

> That is why the real problem of the Christian life comes where people do not usually look for it. It comes the very moment you wake up each morning. All your wishes and hopes for the day rush at you like wild animals. And the first job each morning consists simply in shoving them all back; in listening to that other voice, taking that other point of view, letting that other larger, stronger, quieter life come flowing in. And so on, all day. Standing back from all your natural fussings and frettings; coming in out of the wind.[29]

Is asking for divine help ever like that for you?

In the midst of the chaotic environment that is life, do you find spaces, see space, for divine action? Do you ask for help from an eternal source of social support? In what circumstances? Has support ever been provided in ways you can identify? What kind of response do you expect? Would action that you never see, or action that happens in a way that's different from what you expected, count as a reply?

Invitation to write . . .

....

....

....

....

....

During worship, or at other times when connecting with God, I feel joy which lifts me out of my daily concerns. _____ I feel joy that lifts me out of my daily concerns when experiencing a connection with the divine.
Never (1), Once in a while (2), Some days (3), Most days (4), Every day (5), Many times a day (6)

14

Many of us live a flat life. We hear a droning noise as we go about our activities. Do we only feel joy when something amazing happens, or can we find bursts of joy all around us as we live out each day? Feeling joy is not the same as being happy. Joy has a transcendent nature and can also feel serious. It doesn't just distract us from our problems or distract us from boredom. It lifts us up.

Some examples of this experience of joy from interviews include

- "When listening to certain kinds of music, I feel ecstatic, a divine connection."
- "Being silent in a very old building with high ceilings can be uplifting to me."

- "My concerns fade into the background when I am singing religious music with others."
- "When standing on a hillside looking out."
- "When I see the success of others and feel excited by their success."
- "When I am working outside, and look up and see light in the sky through the clouds, I realize more what matters, and my troubles fade."
- "During an Irish funeral wake, and the celebration surrounding that time."

We get bogged down in daily tasks. Worries about what will happen can absorb us. Even the most well-intentioned worries about the state of the world can bog us down. But we can also feel joy. We can be charged with transcendence.

Music can be transporting for me. Think of a piece of music that you find personally uplifting. Our tastes in music can be very different. But the end result can be a joy that lifts us out of our daily concerns. I find that Monteverdi's *Vespers* and many pieces by Mozart do this for me, but also a wide variety of more modern music—Matisyahu, the Hasidic rapper; for example, some jazz trumpet music; Mumford and Sons' *The Cave*, or the live version of *In the Morning* by Nina Simone. I went to a Yeasayer concert this past year. Their music is not necessarily "spiritual," but I find much of it joyful, touching on ultimate connection. Being at the concert with others, up close and personal in the small club in Cleveland while listening to the band, various lyrics caught me, and the beat lifted me out of a funk. The enthusiasm of some of the band members was contagious.

Enthusiasm comes from the Greek for "god" and "within." What kinds of experiences light the fire of the divine within us? We tend to drift toward a self-focus in our daily routines, and caring for others can take us out of that. But the arts can also powerfully orient us outward, and, no matter what the intention of the artists, can deepen our connection with the divine. Great art, such as a Van Gogh celebration of bright color in a landscape, or a Kandinsky painting full of color and excitement, can bring joy.

When I originally designed this item, it was to address the sense of exhilaration or joy felt, for example, when we are singing together with others in a worship setting or praying in a group. In those settings we can "lose ourselves," lose the fretting self, the part of us weighed down by life. I was trying to capture both personal joy and that felt in collective celebrations. Singing "Silent Night" in a candlelit service on Christmas Eve (tidings of comfort and joy!), or clapping and belting out gospel music in a lively charismatic gathering, are kinds of experiences that fit here. For some, the most intense spiritual experiences happen when in group settings such as these, and feelings here can be intensified.

All sorts of places can encourage this kind of joy in us, this access to an awareness that we are fully alive—from websites and videos to the design of objects and interiors. There is a great video online of some young urban guys in the rain at a run-down street corner in Oakland, California. They just start to dance, first one, then the others, one at a time until they're all dancing together— the most beautiful creative movement, and in their movement expressing connection with each other.[30] It brought joy to me to watch it. We can transcend the mundane. We have access to a transcendent sense of ourselves through music and other art forms. We can become more ourselves, rather than just trying to be distracted.

When do you feel profound joy? Note some times when you might have had transcendent experiences that lift you out of preoccupation with your troubles. Situations and circumstances may open the door for you to experience the divine while you're together with other people. If so, what are they?

Invitation to write . . .

....

....

....

....

15

I feel thankful for my blessings. ____
Never (1), Once in a while (2), Some days (3),
Most days (4), Every day (5), Many times a day (6)

You'd think this would be an easy one. But somehow it's not—for most of us, anyway. We may even think it's a good idea. But do we do it?

Good things happen to us each day, and we just miss them. Too busy with the activities of daily life, we often just don't notice them. Even in the midst of trials, good things occur. Do we even recognize them? What keeps us from noticing blessings?

Here are some examples from interviews in response to this item:

- "When I say thanks for the food before meals."
- "When I am aware of the sufferings of others, it reminds me of all my blessings."

- "Each morning I express thanks for the love my parents have shown me."
- "When I recite the psalms, the words of thanks and praise bring it out in me."
- "After I recovered from a bad cold, I was so thankful to be able to actually taste food again. The flavor of tomatoes."
- "I am constantly aware that life is a gift rather than something owed to me, and this can affect how I approach things as they emerge throughout the day—the feeling that comes out is thankfulness."
- "I came close to dying and began to more clearly realize all the things I really appreciate in life, and that has made me thankful more each day."

So often we do not savor the obviously good things in our lives. An exercise from the Ignatian Christian tradition is the "*examen* of consciousness," recommended before bedtime. One way of doing this is to take the day just past and roll through it in your mind like a film. The *examen* was designed to reflect on our spiritual journey in a religious context. But many have found that if we start this exercise with an appreciative look at the day, it stretches this practice. It has been effective for my students who are not Christian. When I do this for myself, I go through the day in very slow motion and look for the good things that happened, the blessings. As I move through my memories in this way, the things that I need to examine more deeply bubble to the surface in a gentle yet compelling way. The things that challenge me are put in the context of blessings and it changes the way I see them.

This "thankful for my blessings" question lends itself well to tracking over time. Robert Emmons, a researcher who studies gratitude, found that if people listed things they were grateful for each day, their happiness levels increased by 25 percent.[31] You could follow this particular Daily Spiritual Experience question over time by listing various blessings each day, or just counting them by giving yourself a frequency score on the question.

A poem by William Stafford describes how blessings in the day can sometimes feel for me:

> Just lying on the couch and being happy.
> Only humming a little, the quiet sound in the head.
> Trouble is busy elsewhere at the moment, it has
> so much to do in the world.
>
> People who might judge are mostly asleep; they can't
> monitor you all the time, and sometimes they forget.
> When dawn flows over the hedge you can
> get up and act busy.
>
> Little corners like this, pieces of Heaven
> left lying around, can be picked up and saved.[32]

What is a blessing, after all? Is it only when things seem to be going well for us? The Danish existentialist Søren Kierkegaard wrote, "Life can only be understood backwards, but it must be lived forwards."[33] Many things that happen to us are seen as problems and difficulties when they happen. But when we look back on them, we discover that they were blessings after all. Some things really are blessings in disguise.

Do you ever see blessings buried in more superficial problems? Even in very tough times there is good to be discovered. The things you note, or count, as you answer this DSES question may be obviously good, or they may be things from the past that you now see as good after all. Gratitude is not a simple feeling. Can you identify some things that seemed to be bad at the time but now have worked out quite well?

Chronic dissatisfaction with things as they are, or with myself as I am, can be debilitating. Wanting what is not, keeping us from the joy of what is. I have had the pleasure of knowing people with severe disabilities who experience a full life—life to the full in the midst of limited mobility, chronic pain, or serious cognitive deficits. They often embarrass me with their contentment, when I find myself moaning about my problems. A recent study of people with "locked in" syndrome (where you cannot move, but are still aware of what is going on) has shown that frequently their "quality of life" or happiness scores are high.[34] This is not to say that I would choose that way of living, but it makes me more appreciative of the blessings I have. Not only can we see blessings in the obvious, but also hiding in places we do not expect.

What did you think of when you answered this question? What kinds of things do you find yourself being thankful for? List as many as you can think of. You may want to draw from the distant past as well as your current life.

Invitation to write . . .

....

....

....

....

....

....

16

I feel deep inner peace or harmony. ___
Never (1), Once in a while (2), Some days (3),
Most days (4), Every day (5), Many times a day (6)

I don't chill out easily. I describe myself as "naturally caffeinated." I don't know why this is. It could be genetics, personal history, or upbringing. I look at photos of myself as a crawling toddler, and I look concerned. But that doesn't mean that I don't ever experience "deep inner peace." We can experience this even when our surfaces are disturbed or agitated—a deep sense of assurance, grounded somehow, anchored.

Moments of deep inner peace can happen often in daily life, even when we are tense or full of doubts. We don't have to be sitting in a yoga class or in a prayerful posture to have this experience. (In fact, these kinds of activities may not have a peaceful effect on us.) Finding deep inner peace is a challenge in the hectic lives most of us live. Even when the external noise and busyness are quelled, we still have the voices in our heads—your mother's voice reminding you to clean your room; my father's voice calling me lazy or telling me to buck up; voices generated by the media demanding that we buy, do, perform. Sometimes we can ignore these demands, voices, expectations—for just a moment. This moment of stillness is so worth it. We then have inner space.

This kind of peace is found, not created, and we can find it in all sorts of inner and outer environments.

In the interviews while developing the DSES, people mentioned experiencing deep inner peace during times of contemplative prayer or while meditating, but also at other times. One woman who had been repeatedly treated for clinical depression said that she could have this feeling even when she was very depressed. It was just not as vivid and took more energy to pay attention to it. A young man mentioned that he could experience this even when he was anxious, but maybe not as vividly. This point is important in answering this question. Finding deep inner peace does not necessarily mean feeling calm, happy, or in a good mood.

Deep inner peace does not deny the anxieties we all feel. Life itself, if we are fully living it, provokes some anxiety. But we can still find an inner resting place. For some people this peace question might connect with that idea of *hypostasis* I mentioned earlier, resting in your fundamental self, connected to the divine source. Another Greek concept, *hesychasm*, ἡσυχασμός, captures this, too. It means divine rest, resting in the energy of God, or resting in God's love.

In some ways this seems opposite to what we usually think of as being "jazzed." But maybe we need to redefine what jazzes us. Mihaly Csikszentmihalyi named a concept to describe being in the midst of an activity we love, getting lost in it. He called it "flow." I love to draw and paint. When I am doing those activities I am not fretting, I am wrapped up in the activity in a very pleasant way. I chill. It is not at all dull.

This sense of deep inner peace can also be a signal that I look for to indicate that I am moving in the right direction, making a good decision, in harmony with the divine. One person reported experiencing this when he had done something he felt was right, in the midst of inner struggle. He felt an integrity that left him feeling somehow at ease. Maybe something like an easy conscience. He depended on having this sense in his life as a kind of guidepost.

In describing the music of the composer Arvo Pärt, the designer Gideon Kremer said, "It's a cleansing of all the noise that surrounds us." Certain music definitely helps us experience inner stillness. Music is a powerful way into this for many people. The particular kind of music that can do this is so different, depending on a person's age, culture, religious background. Sometimes religious music does this, but often other music creates the environment for deep inner peace. Some examples of music people have mentioned to me in this context are Arvo Pärt's *Spiegel im Spiegel*, harp music, Gregorian chant, reggae, Debussy's *Clair de Lune*, electronic dance music, and jazz piano, such as Keith Jarrett's *Köln Concerts*. This question asks about the experience of "deep inner peace or harmony." Does the harmony of music ever help to elicit harmony in you?

Before going on with this section, pause here to write. What kinds of things help you find a sense of deep inner peace? Does music do this for you? If so, what kinds?

Invitation to write . . .

....

....

....

....

....

....

Our bodies can help or hinder us in our ability to find moments of inner peace in daily life. My undergraduate students are often stressed out, and they want to experience peace in their lives. In my classes, students seem to be able to experience a sense of deep inner peace when doing breath- and body-focused exercises that bring them more fully into the present moment, fully inhabiting their bodies, paying attention to their breathing rather than the internal noise of their minds.

Although experiences of peace can happen anywhere, certain environments can help. Blocking street noise, or "fasting" from phones, computer/Internet/television can help. Finding a place in the house where you are undisturbed is a good idea (even if it has to be the bathroom!). Going out to find environments that are good for you—a quiet church, mosque, or temple—can be a way to jump-start peacefulness, just as we jump-start an engine. Or the right place for you may be a natural environment—park, backyard, seaside, lake, or river. Water can be particularly helpful. Even after leaving these environments, the peaceful residue can cling to you as you return to the noise. I know that when I come back from time spent in silence on retreat, I am able to experience this more often in the midst of the hustle and bustle of daily life.

Remind yourself again of those words of Julian of Norwich: "All will be well." Be at ease with life as it is, comfortable with the big picture not necessarily in a superficial way, but in a more fundamental and sustaining way. This, too, is a way of experiencing deep inner peace.

When do you experience deep inner peace, if at all? Are there things you do or places you go that help you feel this? Do these feelings signal anything to you? Describe these feelings.

Invitation to write . . .

....

....

....

Now that you've worked through the questions and your experiences in depth, you can either continue on with Part Three, "Why Numbers?," and look at how to interpret your numbers in the context of the scientific uses of the scale; or, if you prefer, move directly to Part Four, "Themes," and explore some aspects of your life using a few of the themes that underlie the sixteen questions.

PART THREE
Why Numbers?

4 Using the Number Scores

I always find that statistics are hard to swallow and
impossible to digest. The only one I can ever remember
is that if all the people who go to sleep in church were laid end to
end they would be a lot more comfortable.
—Mrs. Robert A. Taft (nee Martha Wheaton Bowers)

The Limits of Numbers

Full disclosure here: I think that the process of answering the questions is more important than the number scores themselves. I was even tempted to omit this numbers chapter entirely. Blasphemy for a scientist! Although numbers are useful tools, they are quite crude compared with the fine descriptions of your experiences that you reflected on in the previous chapter. I continue to find that the conversation the items open up between people and the self-explorations they can lead to surpass the utility of the numerical scores.

You have the option to ignore this numbers chapter altogether, if you absolutely hate playing with numbers. The sixteen questions are helpful in and of themselves as a tool for self-understanding and enhancement of your spirituality and in communicating with others. You don't need to think that much about totaling and averaging scores. Answering the questions and giving yourself a frequency score on each one is still valuable, even if you never use the numbers to do anything else.

Numbers have many limits. For example, your score is affected by your level of sensitivity. We can cultivate our sensibilities concerning spiritual experiences, but we'll still have different patterns of experience just because of different levels of sensitivity.

Another issue involving numbers is that to give our experiences a frequency number, we need to place them in a category. Some of us will be more critical, more scrupulous, in the assignment of the category. We are deciding whether to put experience A into category X, sorting beans into containers. And we may decide differently even when the experience may be the same. I may be too scrupulous in what I consider "selfless caring for others" and not put feelings as easily in that category, even though the wording of the question was designed to keep us from being excessively scrupulous about that. We are limited by our language, and the numbers can exaggerate those limitations.

We need to remember the limits of numerical scores in describing our experiences. But as scientists we can't function without numbers, and they do have value, so let's see what we can learn from them.

How to Use the Numbers in Your Life

There are benefits to taking the richness of experience, distilling it into numbers, and using those numbers in various ways. One reason that scientists like numbers is that they allow us to compare things, and see differences and similarities. You can be a scientist by using your numbers to see what the results from research might imply for your life.

Those who use this scale in research total up the numbers for all the questions or use an average score. They compare this with numbers from other sets of questions that measure things like health, happiness, psychological strengths or weaknesses, relationship qualities, feelings, and behaviors. Most researchers find that the set of sixteen questions measures one basic underlying thing. But this does not reduce the need to also look closely at scores for individual questions or groups of them. These can highlight specific kinds of spiritual experiences with special importance and significant implications for particular individuals.

The DSES has been included in surveys of thousands of people in the United States, the General Social Surveys administered by the National Science Foundation. These surveys included a random sampling of people of all cultures, races, parts of the country, ages, and genders. I am not going to include all the results from these in this book—you can always look them up in the scientific papers.[1] But it is worth mentioning that, while a substantial number of people have these experiences many times a day, there is also a spread of the frequencies, with lots of people being in the middle, some having none of these experiences. And many people show great variability between responses for the different questions, with high frequencies on some and low frequencies on others. So no matter what your scores, you fit right in!

When developing the scale, I limited it to only sixteen questions, so that it would be easy to take and administer. The DSES is reasonably short—it takes little more than two minutes to answer the sixteen items for most people (unless you do all the writing that you did in the last chapter!). Now that you have your number scores, you have a benchmark to use for examining your responses over time. (The full scale on one page can be found in the Appendix at the end of this book. You can enter in your number responses from Chapter 3, or just answer it again at this time if you would like to see a total or average score.)

Remember that your total score does not measure how spiritual you are. For example, you may have one or two items where you are really off the charts. There is a ceiling effect in this limited numbered scale—"Many times a day" is the maximum number score. You may be "off the scale" in the intensity and frequency of your feelings of gratitude, for example, and this may in itself provide great richness to your days, even though you score very low on other items. Also the spectrum of *spirituality* extends beyond the answers to these questions.

Another point is that sometimes we have dry patches when we rarely have any of these experiences. That does not mean we are not spiritual or religious. But it tells us something about life. Is this low frequency of experiences connected to other things in our lives? By reviewing the numbers we can learn from and be aware of this in a more explicit way.

Compare Your Scores with Yourself Rather Than Comparing Your Scores with Others

The most fruitful way to use these scores, in my opinion, is not by comparing your scores with those of others, but by observing your scores over time—that is, comparing yourself with yourself. This strategy is being used more and more in the social and medical sciences because scientists see an increasing value in examining "individual differences." Your scores will probably change over time, and the numbers will help you identify these changes and connect them with other things in your life.

You may wish to pick one question, or a small group of questions, to follow or examine in your own life. These may be ones you would especially like to look out for, cultivate, and have more of in your life. By looking at subgroups of items and individual item scores you can address particular questions that are of special importance to you. Increases in particular item scores will increase your overall average score, too, so following the total can work as well. But you may just wish to pick three or four that you see potential for increasing in your life and follow those in particular.

You could also focus on becoming aware of one item or area for one week, and then move on sequentially through the list. Since you are the scientist here, you can choose. There may be spiritual experiences that you don't have so often but would like to cultivate.

You can also look at Part Four, "Themes," to select some subgroups of items that represent themes you may wish to look at more closely in your own life using number scores. Chapter 6, "The Flow of Love," for example, discusses how the flow of love includes "love in" and "love out," and particular questions that highlight that dynamic. You could track the four questions highlighted there (DSES questions numbered 6–9) to examine the balance and flow of love in your life.

If you desire, you can also compare your scores with research study results. Most of the study results that I discuss in the "Studies Have Shown" chapter use the total average score to determine whether spiritual experiences are linked with one or another outcome. Some studies also give results on individual items or groups of items. If you are interested in reading more about survey results on the DSES, you can also read the individual scientific research studies that have been published.[2]

5 "Studies Have Shown"
Results from Research Using the DSES

Our imagination is stretched to the utmost, not, as in fiction,
to imagine things which are not really there, but just to
comprehend those things which are there.
—RICHARD FEYNMAN, PHYSICIST

The Daily Spiritual Experience Scale is being used in scientific studies all over the world. There are over one hundred published studies using the DSES, as well as doctoral and master's theses and hundreds of ongoing studies. They use the questions you have been working with. Many of them use the number scores to help them see other things that spiritual experiences are correlated with. DSES scores predict things in a way that is not just due to chance. We can tell this through statistical tests. All the results I describe in this section are "statistically significant" in this way. When scores correlate in statistically significant ways with other things, like relationship quality, happiness, health, or addictions, this helps to independently confirm the importance and value of spiritual experiences in many people's lives. This is over and above their importance in and of themselves.

I enjoy being involved in research—keeping in touch with a research community in many parts of the world. Last week I had an inquiry from a student working with the scale in Hungary and another from a researcher using a Hindi translation. I have enjoyed working with a researcher in Thailand who wants to find out what helps students make a good transition to college life. It has been fun to help translate the scale into Arabic. For me, it is exciting to think of the many thousands of people who have answered these questions and the effects for them of reflecting on their experience in order to answer the questions. I can't talk to each of those who answer the questions, but I get to read the results.

This section describes some of these results in depth, but here are some key points:

- The set of questions works in lots of cultures, with people of many religious and spiritual backgrounds.
- These experiences are common to many different kinds of people.
- There is evidence that enhancing people's spiritual experiences can enhance their lives, including more positive psychological states and greater well-being and life satisfaction.
- More frequent spiritual experience tends to be linked with greater ability to "bounce back" or greater resiliency in difficult times.
- Spiritual experiences can help with recovery from and prevention of addictions.
- More frequent Daily Spiritual Experiences (DSEs) predict better health behaviors, such as following a healthy diet and adherence to a treatment regimen for cancer.
- More Daily Spiritual Experiences are linked with better relationships with others.
- Some activities designed to have an effect on us spiritually can increase the number and quality of our spiritual experiences.

- The scores are often used in research as an assessment tool to measure changes over time. When people want to know whether what they are doing has had an effect on spirituality as an outcome, they use the scale to measure it.

I taught a course for a number of years called "Understanding and Interpreting Human Studies." It is not easy to go from reading about what a research paper says to figuring out what the implications are for us. The news media often take big leaps from study results to broader conclusions in reporting research results. I was originally a cancer researcher, where I learned firsthand that it is not easy to determine what is the cause and what is the effect, and that there are multiple causes for every effect. One way of trying to isolate particular causes is to "control for" the other variables statistically. Most of the studies described below did that. But when studying messy human beings we just cannot control for everything. We also need to take into account individual differences and subgroup variations: Not all research applies to me in particular. It describes a group as a whole.

Great scientists are cautious about drawing conclusions and aware of all the things they don't know. But there is definitely value in scientific studies—they can tell useful things that we cannot know without research. Here are some of the highlights of studies that tell us something about how Daily Spiritual Experiences correlate with a variety of other interesting things in life.[1]

Relationships

Solid research supports the assertion that more Daily Spiritual Experiences predict better relationships with others. This may be evidence of the "flow of love" in operation, a topic addressed in greater depth in Chapter 6. A study of how spouses help one another out following one spouse's traumatic injury showed that those with more frequent Daily Spiritual Experiences tended to provide more help to their partner. It was the strongest predictor of helping of all the factors studied.[2] A study of a variety of spiritual and religious factors and their effects on marriage found that Daily Spiritual Experiences were linked with marital happiness for both men and women.[3] And in a study of 487 African American couples, more frequent Daily Spiritual Experiences predicted better marital quality for the person themselves, and higher levels of satisfaction with the marriage for both the person and the spouse. This result was independent of attendance at religious services. DSEs were a very strong predictor of marital quality overall.[4]

A study of 497 people showed that those with more Daily Spiritual Experiences were less lonely and had more close friends.[5] Older people with more frequent DSEs were also more "socially integrated," a factor associated with decreased stress.[6] In another study, Daily Spiritual Experiences seemed to help those who had lost a significant person in their lives; even though they were still sad, the loss damaged them less.[7]

In a random group of 1,340 people the DSES strongly predicted informal helping behaviors and giving to charity.[8] In another group of people in midlife, more frequent Daily Spiritual Experiences also predicted more helping behaviors, especially toward strangers. Although the effect was true for those with religious affiliations, it was also pronounced among people who do not belong to a religious community, showing that this set of questions may point to spiritual motivations for helping among people who are not conventionally religious.[9]

Males and Females

Do males and females differ in scores on spiritual experiences? In studies worldwide (Hong Kong, France, Mexico, and the Basque Country, for example), men and women get similar total scores. However, in the United States men tend to report slightly less frequent spiritual experiences overall than women. Why might this be the case? There is an emotional aspect to some of the items. It may be more acceptable for men to report emotions in some cultures than others. This leads us to ask a follow-up question: Do cultures where men can express emotions also encourage them to be more open to spiritual experiences? Some cultural differences may also reflect the predominant religious influences in a culture, regardless of whether individuals continue to be involved in organized religion, and this may influence gender differences and similarities.

Also, studies have shown that the role of Daily Spiritual Experiences in life can vary for men and women. For college-age men, more frequent spiritual experiences were more highly correlated with a career choice that valued service or influence on social issues, but for women the frequency of DSEs did not correspond with this kind of choice.[10] This makes me wonder what underlies the decision to pursue a more altruistic career, and whether spiritual experiences might weigh more heavily in that choice among men than among women. In a group of urban adolescents, higher DSEs correlated with positive moods for both males and females, but was a significant predictor of life satisfaction especially for males.[11] A study of 615 adolescents showed that DSEs were associated with less depressive symptoms only in the girls.[12] Once again, these results are aggregations of groups, but give us something to think about as we reflect on our own scores, and communicate with people of a different gender.

Various Cultures and Translations

By comparing reports of ordinary spiritual experiences in different cultures we can gain some fascinating insights. For example, studies in Mexico, Brazil, and the Basque region in Europe have shown higher Daily Spiritual Experiences than in the United States overall. A study in the Basque Country, an area in the Pyrenees between France and Spain, showed higher rates of DSEs among atheists than among religious people.[13]

Cultures do not always follow political or language boundaries; countries encompass multiple cultures. There are a number of ongoing studies of Hispanics and African Americans, for example, that are showing particular patterns in those communities. I recently received a request to include the DSES in the National Children's Study, which will follow 100,000 pregnant women and their offspring over many years. One of the reasons they gave for using the scale was to examine how spiritual experience might be particularly helpful for certain ethnic groups in coping with life stressors.

The many translations help researchers explore cultural variations and commonalities, and demonstrate the ongoing use of the scale in many different countries. I especially enjoy working on translations. At the time of this writing, there are more than thirty translations of the scale, and the psychometric properties of the DSES have been published in Spanish, French, Mandarin Chinese, Portuguese (Brazil), and German. Other translations in use include Arabic, Dutch, Filipino, Finnish, Flemish, Greek, Hebrew, Hindi, Hungarian, Indonesian, Italian, Korean, Lithuanian, Malay, Nigerian, Persian, Polish, Romanian, Russian, Portuguese (Portugal), Serbian, Thai, Turkish, Urdu, Vietnamese, and Zuni Pueblo.

Burnout, Workplace Issues, and Leadership Styles

Resiliency, the ability to bounce back, is such a useful quality to have. In every work environment there are people and circumstances that can drain us over time. We want to be resilient and not burn out. The Daily Spiritual Experiences you have been reflecting on have real potential to help prevent burnout, providing some extra resources in the midst of difficult times.

This holds true across nations and cultures. The Chinese translation of the DSES was used in a study of 245 professional and support staff in a hospital in Hong Kong. More frequent Daily Spiritual Experiences predicted less anxiety, depression, and total burnout.[14] Among Protestant ministers in Germany, many of whom were prone to burnout, more Daily Spiritual Experiences were linked with less burnout.[15] In a study in the United States, more frequent spiritual experiences lessened physical, mental, and emotional forms of burnout among professional end-of-life caregivers.[16] Spiritual experiences had a protective effect against fatigue and exhaustion.

Teachers in Nigeria with higher DSEs had less work-family conflict.[17] Teachers in England with higher DSEs reported having more inner resources and finding deeper meaning in their work.[18] A recent study of 854 employees found that after looking at many religious and spiritual variables, only Daily Spiritual Experiences predicted positive workplace outcomes.[19]

Other effects of DSEs in the workplace continue to be explored as the DSES is included in studies conducted by schools of management in the United States and abroad. Leaders with higher DSEs were less likely to be rated as passive-avoidant by their peers.[20] And people with higher DSEs engaged in fewer negative interpersonal and organizational behaviors—including questionable ethical actions—than people who had lower DSEs, even when controlling for job stress and job satisfaction.[21]

Healthy Behaviors and Health

Looking after yourself is an important part of physical health, particularly for those who are ill. But health-promoting behaviors, like exercising, eating well, and stopping smoking, are often hard to do. In a study of 167 young adults diagnosed with cancer, religious attendance had little impact on health behaviors, while Daily Spiritual Experiences were linked to greater performance of health behaviors.[22] The young people with higher Daily Spiritual Experiences tended to eat better, take their medications more regularly, and get more sleep.

What motivates us to care for ourselves well, and why is Daily Spiritual Experience linked with this? In a study of heart failure, DSEs were connected to "self-efficacy," a sense that we can make a difference.[23] Recently, some research headlines asked, "Does God make you fat?" Daily Spiritual Experiences, although not a diet aid per se, have been shown to be linked with positive health behaviors that include eating well. And there is some preliminary support linking increased DSEs to weight loss.[24] The kinds of experiences identified in the DSES can help us to feel that we can be effective in our lives, and this is important for our ability to change our behaviors.

A study of Lithuanian college students showed a significant relationship between higher DSEs and wellness for males and females.

They also found that females who have more Daily Spiritual Experiences paid more attention to physical health issues (engaging in physical activity and maintaining a healthy diet), were more creative and active, were more resilient in the face of stress, had stronger gender and cultural identity, and gave priority to positive self-care. Overall, spirituality had a significant positive impact on the health-oriented lifestyles of students.[25] A study of African Americans demonstrated that individuals who scored high on the DSES had lower HIV risk behaviors.[26]

In a study of 811 older patients, more frequent DSEs predicted fewer days of long-term hospital care, as well as better physical and psychological health.[27] Another study examining 6,534 older adults found more frequent Daily Spiritual Experiences linked to better self-reported health.[28] Daily Spiritual Experiences were positively linked with health in the cross-sectional random sample General Social Survey, no matter what the level of public religious activity.[29] More frequent DSEs were also linked with better health in a study in France.[30]

Pain

Nobody likes pain. Some pain really causes us to suffer; other pain, not so much. For example, a brief injury hurts, but we do not suffer as much as we might with chronic back pain, even though the intensity of the back pain may be less. A daily diary study of pain among arthritis patients tracked both DSEs and pain scores. DSEs in that study were connected with more positive mood and lower negative mood over the course of the study.[31]

Researchers studying the effects of meditation on pain tolerance compared a spiritual meditation group with a secular meditation group. They measured pain tolerance by how long participants could keep their hand immersed in ice-cold water. Following the spiritual meditation, but not the secular meditation, over a period of weeks, pain tolerance improved, along with more frequent Daily Spiritual Experiences.[32] The people who used spiritual meditation could keep their hands in the ice water longer, showing higher pain tolerance, and they also reported more Daily Spiritual Experiences.

On the other hand, occasionally DSEs can be higher in those who have disability, disease, and pain than in those who are healthy. For example, in another study, more frequent DSEs predicted better mental health, but were correlated with higher pain scores.[33] One reasonable way of interpreting this data is to think that the disease can push us to draw on transcendent resources, pay more attention to the big picture, the "more than," to better cope with the physical distress.

Addictions: Drug and Alcohol Abuse

It is not a coincidence that alcohol is referred to in the English language as "spirits." The more Daily Spiritual Experiences we have, the less of other "spirits" we may need. By focusing on the excitement and joys of daily life found in awareness of the spiritual aspects of life, we may need less stimulation through addictive substances. Also, various spiritual experiences that are comforting and soothing can calm us more effectively and with fewer side effects than addictive substances can. I love a good cup of coffee and, at other times, a glass of wine or beer, but the patterns of behavior that are addressed here are ones that cause grief to people themselves and the people they relate to.

The DSES has been used in a number of studies of alcohol and drug abuse. Following a group of 123 alcoholics over the course of treatment showed that more frequent Daily Spiritual Experiences predicted that people would not relapse after six months following the treatment.[34] Spiritual experiences, but not religious affiliation, predicted positive treatment outcomes in a Jewish faith-based residential substance-abuse treatment center.[35] A study of another group of 198 alcoholics showed that the whole set of DSES questions predicted staying sober for longer, and this was also true for both the subgroup of questions with the word *God* and the subgroup without. In this study the DSES was also correlated with more helping behaviors.[36]

Happiness and Life Satisfaction

If you are interested in having more Daily Spiritual Experiences, you probably think that they will improve your life. While these experiences represent something worth having on their own, it would be nice if they also increased your happiness. Research evidence using the DSES suggests that they do. The General Social Survey data shows a strong positive association between more frequent DSEs and more happiness, excitement with life, self-esteem, and optimism. These links were there no matter what age, socioeconomic status, gender, or ethnic group respondents belonged to.[37]

Links have also been shown between DSEs and greater well-being or life satisfaction in various studies with groups as diverse as widows and widowers, French adults, inner-city elders, prison inmates, and adolescents.[38] The connections to positive emotions and well-being remain even after accounting for personality and other religious factors.[39] An interesting study of people from Mexico and the Basque region of Europe showed positive links with life satisfaction and psychological well-being, regardless of personality type. A group of arthritis sufferers reported more energy when they had more frequent DSEs.[40] A study of a diverse group of urban youth showed better psychological adjustment and less distress among those with more frequent DSEs, and more frequent DSEs correlated with positive emotional states.[41]

Less Stress, Depression, and Anxiety

Research shows that while depressed people can have frequent spiritual experiences, more frequent DSEs generally predict fewer depressive symptoms.[42] Groups showing less depression with higher DSEs include adolescents, heart attack victims, survivors of domestic violence, and those suffering from arthritis. In a study of parents, fathers with higher frequencies of spiritual experiences reported lower levels of depressive symptoms than those with lower frequencies of spiritual experience.[43] Chronic disease can easily lead to depression, but it led to even more depression in a group of older adults with fewer spiritual experiences, who were followed for two years in a continuing care retirement community.[44] And in a study of physically isolated older people, those with more frequent Daily Spiritual Experiences were less depressed.[45] A study of 200 elderly Korean immigrants in New York City found that more frequent DSEs were linked with less depression.[46]

Studies have also shown less anxiety among those with more frequent Daily Spiritual Experiences, both in the United States and other countries.[47]

In a study of 244 older adults, DSEs seemed to enable those with high stress in their lives to have less negative moods—this is called "stress buffering." DSEs also had a direct effect on positive mood, and these effects happened regardless of the individual's religious orientation.[48]

Emotional resilience is something we all would like more of. Bad things happen; situations are not always ideal. A variety of religious and spiritual variables were examined in a study of 273 young adults raised in families with high levels of depression in the parents. This environment can often cause depression in the young adults. Only one aspect of spirituality/religiousness predicted resilience—Daily Spiritual Experiences. The young adults with higher DSEs were better protected from the effects of the family environment.[49] Higher DSEs predicted less distress and more post-traumatic growth following bereavement.[50]

Spirituality as an Outcome, an End in Itself

How do we measure spirituality? In my academic publications over the years and in this book, I have emphasized that the Daily Spiritual Experience Scale is just one part of the complex aspect of life that we call *spirituality*. Nevertheless, people often want to enhance spirituality, or spiritual sensitivity, and use the DSES as one way to see if they have done it. The DSES is being used as an "outcome" measure for various projects. It is probably the best single scale out there to do this in multicultural settings. The DSES is sensitive to change over time, which makes it especially suitable for measuring whether a particular training program, treatment, or activity has had an effect on spirituality. Researchers, therapists, and individuals can measure rates of DSEs before and after these activities.

A control group study of the effects of two one-day spiritual retreats on nurses' spirituality in a group of 199 critical care nurses showed more frequent DSEs at the end of the retreat and even six months after it.[51] A study investigating face-to-face prayer for patients with depression and anxiety showed that DSES scores

increased and remained high a month following the prayer intervention.[52] A study of spiritual direction in substance abuse populations showed increases in DSES scores.[53] And an online program
designed to cultivate sacred moments used a control group who
wrote daily about their lives.[54] Both groups, even the one with
people who just wrote about their lives, increased Daily Spiritual
Experience frequency over the course of the experiment and six
weeks afterward. A study of mindfulness stress reduction showed
that DSEs increased over time during that study, with results lasting a year after the study.[55]

In a more holistic approach to medical care, outcomes can
include more than physical improvements. This is especially true
in chronic disease and at end of life. In these cases, spiritual outcomes may be one goal of treatment. This was part of the rationale
behind the World Health Organization project mentioned earlier.
The Daily Spiritual Experience Scale has also been included in a
textbook on nursing assessments and a Canadian holistic medicine outcomes database.[56] It measures a feature of life worth paying attention to in the context of a broader definition of health.
And the DSES has been acknowledged in published studies as a
good tool for assessment in counseling.[57]

Work in Progress

Recently I have been helping organizations that provide residential
care for abused and neglected children and adolescents to assess
the effects of the spiritual dimension of their work. The DSES is
being used in these environments as an assessment of outcomes
for the young people and those who care for them. It is also being
used as an outcome measure in a variety of religious settings and
in secular programs like Outward Bound, to assess some effects

of the programs. There are hundreds of ongoing studies using the scale. I get three to four e-mails a week from people who register to use it. For example, it is being used in studies of post-traumatic stress disorder in veterans, burnout in humanitarian workers in Malaysia and China. In Italy and the United States, it is being used to study how traumatic events can lead to personal growth for some people, something called "post-traumatic growth." In the field, the DSES is being used in social work, health settings, end-of-life care, addiction treatment, faith-based organizations, and pastoral care. Doctoral and master's students use the DSES in their dissertations in fields as diverse as clinical psychology, social work, religious studies, exercise science, ecology, ministry, business studies, and occupational therapy.

What Are Some Implications for You?

What most interests you in these research results? What has most relevance for your life and your communication with others? Are there any special implications for you? Most of these studies use an item total, or an item average, of all the questions on the scale. That is because, for researchers, they all "hang together" psychometrically. That means they all measure the same underlying concept, and that is what the researchers are interested in. You have the freedom to select a few questions to focus on or to look at the whole group of items. However, it may be useful for you to know that the research results support continuing to examine the scale as a whole.

Look through the list of research results just described and decide which of those are most important to you personally: health behaviors, relationships, burnout, stress buffering, improvements in daily mood, life satisfaction?

You can see that the spiritual experiences you have been exploring in the sixteen questions are generally connected with a variety of good things. This is a result that much of the research has in common. If we have spiritual experiences, noticing them and treasuring them can affect our scores. Over time, changes in our attitudes and the way we live our lives have the potential to influence our perception of our relationship with the divine. Another important implication of the research is that these experiences occur frequently in many countries, cultures, and age groups, and among both religious and nonreligious groups. There is something we have in common here, something we can share with one another in the midst of the richness and variety of our particular lives. Hopefully, this will help us to understand one another better and share something important about ourselves with others.

PART FOUR
Themes

We hear a musical theme in various forms during a long piece of music. Or we can have a three-course meal based on a Mediterranean theme, and as we eat our way through it we can become more aware of the Mediterranean nature of the flavors and influences. So, too, there are underlying themes in the set of sixteen questions.

The details of our lives influence the kinds of underlying patterns we perceive. And our concepts of the world influence the details we notice and how we interpret them. In the following chapters we will be clarifying certain themes and concepts, to better nest our experiences in a coherent framework for easier and more useful access. The metaphors we use influence what and how we see.[1] And our experiences of awe, love, gratitude, and peace can influence the patterns and underlying character that we find in life.

We sometimes miss the forest for the trees. In Chapters 6 through 9 we have a chance to focus on the forest. Here, too, as in Chapter 3, taking the time to write about each theme, talk with others about it, or dictate comments into your phone can help your understanding as well as strengthen relationships. These themes can reveal significant things about our lives. "The Flow of Love" and "Connection versus Alienation" are interlinked but worth considering separately. "Yes!" describes an affirmation of life that resonates throughout the questions. And the last theme, "Translating 'God,'" explores further how you and others "translate" the word God or envision the concept of the divine as explored in the sixteen questions.

6 The Flow of Love

This is what we mean by the term spiritual: It is the ecstatic force that stirs all our goals. When we perceive it, it is as if our mind were gliding for a while with an eternal current.
—ABRAHAM JOSHUA HESCHEL

Who isn't interested in love? We give love, we receive love: It has a flowing quality. The kind of love addressed in the spiritual experience questions is freely given, sustaining, upbuilding love, called by some "compassionate love." Not only does this refer to compassion for those who are suffering, but also to love that helps the loved one to flourish. This love occurs with strangers as well as in families, marriages, and romantic relationships, and with friends. One of the best descriptions I've heard of this kind of love is, "To set aside one's own agenda for the sake of, to strengthen, or to give life to the other."[1]

This kind of love centers on the good of the other. It's the kind of love that feels so good to be on the receiving end of. Good in a lasting way, one that sticks to the ribs and doesn't give indigestion. It is a caring love that has a weight, a nourishing quality. To be loved when it is the choice of the other, and at some cost emotionally or physically, can make a special impact.[2]

Becoming acutely aware of moments of love in our daily lives is not always easy. Try the following exercise.

Recalling Love: An Exercise in Three Parts

1. Close your eyes. Pay attention to your breath moving in . . . moving out, long and deep, with the air going into your abdomen, and then out fully, for five breaths.

2. Reflect on an ordinary moment in the past when you gave of yourself to another at a cost. It might have been a small gesture, or something with a higher profile. The cost might have been in time, energy, emotions, money—beyond what was expected of you. The person might have been someone close to you or a stranger. Move through that moment in your imagination. What did it feel like? Rest in that moment. Give yourself a while to fully revisit this in your memory.

3. Remember a time in the past when you personally felt truly loved—loved for who you truly are, beyond the momentary circumstances, beyond the superficial. Pick a time that still holds particular importance for you. What were the circumstances of the relationship and its context? Return to this scene and try to relive it. What did this feel like? What was your life like at the time? Experience the event again from the inside out, rather than as an observer from the outside. Smell the smells, hear the sounds. Stay with the scene as long as you experience something of the joy that was yours.

Do this exercise yourself and reflect on your experiences in a relaxed way.

Invitation to write . . .

....

....

....

....

....

....

....

The first time I offered this exercise to others was to a large audience of mostly scientists and academics at MIT. Dr. Cicely Saunders, the founder of the modern hospice movement (which provides places for people to be cared for at the end of life) was in the audience. She was a strong woman in her eighties who had done so much in her life for others. She made a point of coming up to me after the presentation. She talked about how doing the exercise powerfully brought back to her an event from her past when she had been loved, and what a good experience it had been for her to revisit this once again. Some of us give so much in our lives. Taking time to dwell on love flowing in can be very positive and nourishing. It can contribute to the flow of love in our lives.

The four questions in the DSES that specifically focus on love (6–9) can help us attend to this particular kind of experience of love in our lives. I have been involved in developing scientific research on this other-centered love over the years. As you can imagine, it is hard to measure in a satisfactory way. The "I feel a selfless caring for others" item (8) and the "I accept others even when they do things I think are wrong" item (9) from the DSES have been used as one way to measure the giving of this kind of love in a number of scientific studies.[3] And for the flow of love to be complete, we must also receive love. The two additional questions on feeling divine love—God's love—directly or through others (6 and 7) get at this receiving of caring, transcendent love. Although these items focus specifically on love, a number of the other questions also measure connection and support that can fuel our love—the spiritually touched by the beauty of creation item (1), the comfort item (11), and the thankful for my blessings one (15), for example. The flow of love is a crucial part of the aspects of life measured in the entire set of questions.

Love Sweet and Tough

Other-centered love is not all mush and sweetness. Sometimes it is easier to just give in, to give the ones you love whatever they want, but that may not be the best thing for them. An example of this might be how we handle a friend whose behaviors are causing them harm, or harming their relationships. We may seem unsupportive in the short run as we help them to avoid long-term problems. This is one of many reasons we cannot measure love by actions. So when you are "counting" your Daily Spiritual Experiences of love, don't forget to notice those attitudes and actions that desire the best for others so that they will flourish, but are wrapped in a tough disguise. Have you ever found yourself standing firm when a friend wanted to do something you saw as potentially destructive, even in the face of negative feedback from them? ("Friends don't let friends drive drunk.") The love we perceive coming from others may also be hidden, packaged in this way.

Receiving Love: Can the Love Questions Help?

For love to flow, we need balance between giving love and receiving love. I developed a model of love for use in research. The model explicitly incorporates the idea that for love to flow out from us in effective ways, there need to be sources of love in our own lives.[4] If we do not allow love in, we stop the flow. The airplane stewards say, "In case of a decrease in cabin pressure, put on your own oxygen mask before helping a child next to you." If we are not breathing, we are of little use to others.

Burnout is a real issue for those of us involved in caregiving, whether we're professional caregivers, parents caring for a child, adults caring for an elderly parent, or volunteers in various caring roles. We need to make sure that we allow love to flow into our lives. From God directly or from other people—love centered on our flourishing, love flowing in.

The DSES questions you have been working with address two ways that we can experience love flowing in—directly and through others. These can both be important sources of love in our lives. Most religious belief systems, especially those that encourage a personal relationship with a divine being, set up ways to experience God's love directly. They describe a love from God that is always there—we just have to tune in and be willing to be who we are, aware of both our strengths and weaknesses, in the divine presence. If I sometimes accept others, even if they do things I think are wrong, consider how much more God does this. Divine mercy. Aimed at me.[5]

If we use the introductory *God*-translation, and substitute that which represents the divine or holy for us, even more people can say that they can experience divine love directly. Some people have just not been in many situations where others express an other-centered love to them. This is sad. Feeling love depends on that love being expressed in the first place! However, an ever-present divine love is still there to draw on, to fill the tank.

Operating with other people in a tit-for-tat environment does not encourage love to flow freely. If we only give love in order to receive something or we only give when we expect something in return, that does not fuel this divine, other-centered love in our lives. An example of this is when partners in a relationship keep close tally on whether a gift has been reciprocated. We just end up with a balance sheet, a scorecard. This is not a balanced flowing of love, but an accounting spreadsheet. If we give love in this context, we are more likely to see the love we receive in this way, too.

Sometimes other things disguise themselves as love. I worked many years in grant making, giving away a foundation's money for research projects. This was a very strategic activity, and it was crucial to pay attention to what the sources of love were in my life. I had to be vigilant that the positive strokes I received from those I gave money to were not the source of my good feelings about myself. Otherwise, the flow of love out to those in need became tangled up in my own personal needs. I could easily find myself more likely to give money to those who gave me positive strokes, and wise decision making would go down the tubes. I needed to be aware of this dynamic and not allow it to drive my decisions. My own needs for love needed to be filled from somewhere else. And in order to allow love to flow freely, I needed to rise above the "tit-for-tat" metrics. I had to continually find other ways to fuel my love, care, and concern for others.

Does Receiving Divine Love Fuel the Love That Flows Out from You?

Is this flow of love in your life fueled at all by a higher power? W. H. Auden, one of the greatest poets of the twentieth century, wrote about a spiritual experience in his life:

> I felt myself invaded by a power which, though I consented to it, was irresistible and certainly not mine. For the first time in my life I knew exactly—because, thanks to the power, I was doing it—what it means to love one's neighbour as oneself. . . . My personal feelings towards them were unchanged—they were still colleagues, not intimate friends—but I felt their existence as themselves to be of infinite value and rejoiced in it.[6]

I think about love for my daughters and how it feels. I wonder about how it influences their obvious care for each other. Where did it come from? What keeps it going?

An Irish legend about St. Kevin has recently been put into poetic form by Seamus Heaney. (There is a great recording of him reading it.[7]) The legend describes St. Kevin kneeling in his monastic cell, praying with arms outstretched, one out the window through the bars of the cell. A bird settles in his outstretched hand and makes a nest there. Because of his compassion, Kevin just stays in that position until the eggs hatch. It must have been very hard, and he would have become very tired and wanted to stop. Not even reflecting on the logistics, where did he find the energy to continue holding the nest while the eggs hatched? Heaney in his poem touches on the eternal and rooted wellspring of love in the midst of difficulties, and how care for the bird allows that wellspring to flow through Kevin.

Are you holding any birds that have begun to nest? Do you ever find yourself stuck in the midst of commitment and care, in distress yet still desiring to love? Do you find yourself overextended in some way or another? And then what do you do? How do you sustain this love and care? How does that feel?

Invitation to write . . .

....

....

....

....

....

....

There seem to be so many things involved in giving love to others in a way that enables them to flourish. It is different for strangers and for close friends. Bring to mind some specific times you gave of yourself for the good of another person, at a cost. Did this love feel full of affection or passion? Did it take the form of practical kindness? Do you more often have a sense of willing the good of another, a conscious weighing and active decision making? When you love, do you worry? Does it drain you? Do you ever feel resentful? Does it energize you?

Invitation to write . . .

....

....

....

....

....

....

....

Obstacles to Love Flowing In

What are some signals that the flow of love is not working? Resentment can be a signal that the flow of love is out of whack: Love is not flowing freely for us, but has become stuck somehow. It can signal that our motivations are not other-centered in a healthy way, or it may mean that we are not attending adequately to the love flowing into or through us. Burnout is another signal that love is not flowing freely. We may need to find ways to notice or find the love that can flow in and revive us.

Divine love expressed through others, in relationships, is the main source of love for many of us. It depends on there being people around who are willing to express other-centered love to us. But another thing is critical. We need to be attentive—listening for it. Regularly answering the DSES questions on "love in" can help us attend to these expressions of love toward us, as can writing in a journal as we reflect on moments of love from others. Doing the memory exercise described earlier (reliving love in the past) can also help. It is important in our lives that we cultivate an attitude of appreciation that does not disparage the care others express, making sure we put love from others into the category that lets us count it as care and love for us.

Allowing love in requires vulnerability. Are we open to being loved as we are, to being seen clearly, full of flaws, and yet still loved? Do we discount the love of others and of God? Do we think they will only love us if we are perfect? Or can we perceive this accepting love in our lives and allow it to contribute to the flow of love in us? In my own life I often block love coming in, restraining its power. One reason is that I don't trust—other people, God. Another is that I do not want to see myself as needing this love. Another reason is that being open to love from others means that I am not fully "in control." I have not opened myself to receiving a wonderful gift from another.

Mercy

The "I accept others" question (9), which reflects the notion of mercy, is a part of the flow of love, too. The flow of love includes valuing ourselves fundamentally as well as valuing others in that same way. We learn to value ourselves, just as we are, by seeing ourselves reflected in the accepting gaze of another person. We can also learn about this attitude through spiritual writings and practices. That same deep appreciation can spread to our attitudes toward others. Think back to the exercise where you remembered a time that you felt love (at the beginning of this chapter). The power of that love was influenced by the free actions of the other, and his or her valuing of you in a fundamental way, accepting you as you are.

Mercy is not a matter of feeling sorry for people or pitying them. Rather, it is an acceptance that can reach the other like a healing balm.

Compassionate love can be present in people who have no sense of a personal God. Yet, for many, thinking of the divine as a "being" capable of love is critical to the perception of divine love. If we envision ourselves being connected to the divine, connected to others and all of life, this can be strengthening. But there is something powerful about theologies that see persons, including the divine person, as distinct. If my spouse and I were the same person, our love would not be as meaningful to me. There is something beautiful about being a radical other, as well as seeing our connection to each other and a larger whole. Grasping this complexity of connection and distinctness may be critical to seeing more clearly how love works in our lives.

Jessica Powers captures some of this sense of receiving God's love in a fine poem where she pictures herself wandering into the woods and finding peace, not in her achievements or strivings toward perfection, but in the welcome and acceptance and quiet woods of God's mercy. She also speaks of her love as "a fragment of infinite loving and never my own."[8]

Spend some time reflecting on the quality of "love flowing in" in your life. Are there times when love might be there for you but you do not let love in or erect obstacles? Think back to a particular time and reinhabit it. If you do not let love in, can you identify any reasons why you might do this? Then remember a time when you let love in, even a little bit. Are there ways you can see right now to cultivate awareness of divine love in your life? Are there holy valentines coming under your door in small or larger ways in your life?

Invitation to write . . .

....

....

....

....

....

....

Self-Compassion and Self-Acceptance

One thing that is not explicitly contained in these sixteen questions is the issue of divine love and mercy that flows *through you to yourself.* This is hard to tease out in our perceptions of our attitudes. It's not the same as "me-me-me," in a self-centered way, and it is not letting yourself off the hook when you need to be responsible. Sometimes self-compassion is tough love. Self-compassion is part of consciously valuing yourself. Sometimes you are the best person to express care and love for yourself in a way that is "more than." If we envision the divine within us, in ways that many religions and philosophies articulate, we can sing divine love to our own hearts.

Can you accept yourself even when you do things you think are wrong? This doesn't mean being irresponsible, but taking a warm and loving attitude to yourself in the midst of falling short of your aspirations, or when you do something you think is wrong. Some of us need to be reminded not to be harder on ourselves than we are on others. Can you include yourself as one of the "others" that you feel a selfless caring for? A good piece of advice I heard for those who have trouble caring adequately for themselves is to treat themselves as they would a beloved friend. Are you willing to be a conduit of divine love for yourself?

This is part of the flow of love theme that is worth observing in your life, and is especially important for some of us. If this is something that you think you need to pay more attention to, you could include an explicit reminder of this in your notes on the four love questions (6–9). For example, in the "selfless caring for others" question you could put a reminder to consider caring for yourself explicitly as well as others, and you could also explicitly have a reminder about accepting yourself when you answer the question on accepting others.

Balance

Now might be a good time to look at the balance of the flow of love in your life. Look at the subgroup of four love questions (6–9). You might also include some of the other questions that reflect spiritual support and care in your life.

Do they tell you anything about yourself? You need love to flow in both directions—in and out. Is love easier for you to give, or easier for you to receive? Both are important. No love out, and you do not connect to the world around you through giving of yourself and welcoming others, and in the process you too can suffer like a stunted plant. No love in, and you can become burned out, dried up. Getting the balance right keeps the flow going.

Spend some time reflecting on the balance in your own life. Do you have a good balance in your life? Is love flowing?

Invitation to write . . .

....

....

....

....

....

....

7 Connection versus Alienation

We say "far away";
the Zulu has for that a word which means, in our sentence form,
"There where someone cries out: 'O mother, I am lost.'"
—Martin Buber

o one wants to be lonely, even if we sometimes like to be alone. It is written in our bones to want to be connected with others, to be in relationship, to feel close to others.

A Celtic Approach to Spirituality

When I consider desire for closeness to the divine, a sense of God's presence, being spiritually touched by the beauty of creation, being connected to all of life, and finding joy in worship with others, I think of versions of St. Patrick's Breastplate, an ancient Celtic prayer. During my years in Ireland, I found the northern coastal scenery absolutely spectacular. In that sun-starved place with harsh winds from the north, the ocean touches the rock-faced cliffs and the green hills meet the sea. It doesn't surprise me that this prayer arose from that place, especially given the way with words that the Irish have. "God's arms around our shoulders, the fragrance of the Holy Spirit in our nostrils, the conversations of heaven's company on my lips . . . a home for God in my heart." Or: "Christ above me, Christ below me, within me, in those I meet."

Celtic Christianity in its original forms took the connection to all of life that the early Celtic peoples celebrated and found that this could be expressed and enriched in Christian form.

The Daily Spiritual Experience Scale was designed to measure "relationship with the transcendent," so, not surprisingly, the whole set of sixteen items addresses the theme of connection.

Connected to All of Life?

If we ever feel "connected to all of life" (3), just what is it that we feel connected to? Other humans, the grass under our feet as part of the whole of the natural world, life as extending beyond our planet and out into the stars? People in the past and future? All of life colored by religious language, such as God's breath? This question gives us an opportunity to explore connection in a creative way.

The musical group Bowerbirds has a song and video, "In Our Talons," that brings home our connections to each other and all of life in the natural world.[1] It addresses environmental concerns in the context of care for one another. Does connection to all of life connect us to the ground of being, God in the world? Or do we perceive it in a less theistic context? When we feel intimacy with the natural world, does it bring with it a transcendent connection? Feeling your toes in the mud or wiggling in the sand, feeling the wind on your cheek and smelling the scent of burning logs, enjoying the touch of an animal nuzzling into the palm of your hand.

The natural world in and of itself is ephemeral, as we are. Trees die. We will die. Somehow the connection we feel to other people and the natural world must stretch beyond the ephemeral—a spiritual experience, a connection to all of life that somehow transcends our transitory nature. We can see value in all of life that has eternal significance. Some people envision connection with a hidden wholeness, a term used by physicist David Bohm. Others sense connection with Hagia Sophia, Ἁγία Σοφία, Holy Wisdom.

Some religions seem to address the disconnect that we often feel between ourselves and the natural environment better than others. Native American religions, for example, emphasize the connection we have to the earth and living creatures. Hinduism has specific ways of envisioning our connections with animals and encouraging the connection to our own bodies as a part of the natural world. But this connection to the natural world is not absent in Christianity, Judaism, and Islam. Theologians of these traditions continue to creatively articulate how God and nature relate to one another. Franciscan spirituality envisions and describes this connection with all of life effectively and creatively.[2] St. Francis's song addresses "brother sun, sister moon."

All experiences of connection are not the same. We can artificially create an oceanic sense—for example, using hallucinogens—and lose ourselves in this way. This may remind us that such a sense is possible, but I think that without natural links to ordinary life, a cohesive and transcendent framework, and a grounding in the ordinary, the effects are likely to be ephemeral and disorienting. This approach may create openness to the transcendent in daily life or may just create a greater sense of existential loneliness once we are no longer under the influence of the drug.

Do you ever feel connection in the context of the natural world? If so, what is it like for you? When is it most palpable and nourishing for you?

Invitation to write . . .

....

....

....

....

....

Connections with Those Who Are Different from Us

It is natural to feel connected with those in our families, our ethnic group, those in our own country. It is not as natural to feel connections with people who are not like us. Pearl Oliner studied rescuers in the Holocaust and found that those who felt a sense of common humanity with other people were more likely to rescue Jews, rather than just stand by.[3] She found baseline differences between Catholics and Protestants in this regard. Catholics were more likely to have a community sense that extended beyond their own cultural and religious group. This sense of connection with others encouraged care for the others and action on their behalf, even when their own safety was at risk. And the subgroup of Protestants who rescued Jews were more likely to have this sense of common community than the Protestant bystanders. I find myself thinking, how frequently do I feel a connection with those who are not like me?

I attend a church that is very ethnically diverse, and after the service I feel less alienated from the world as a whole. Maybe it's the effect of the religious liturgy and the explicit content. But I also think that when together in a religious setting with such a variety of people, there is a connection with others that influences my life in a positive and concrete way. In our lives we need to be connected to others who are like us and close to us. This is important. But to face the challenges in our increasingly interdependent world, we also need to stretch the limits of our comfort zone to survive and grow.

Do you feel connected with those different from you? When does this happen most?

Invitation to write . . .

Connections with Those Who Are Like Us

Connecting with those who are like us, who share beliefs with us, can powerfully affect our lives in good ways. Experiences at synagogue, church, mosque, temple, or worship in an indigenous tradition can enhance for many a connection with others as well as with God. Singing and chanting with others is a powerful way of connecting, as are kneeling together, listening together, reciting prayers together, and moving together. We can feel a joy in these settings, or just feel strongly connected with those we are with, focusing intently with others on something beyond ourselves, transcending together. A study showed that for a group of those who sang hymns, brain scans demonstrated activation of the area of the brain that was linked with intimate relationships with others.[4]

Durante il culto, o in momenti diversi, quando mi sento in sintonia con Dio, avverto un sentimento di gioia che mi solleva dalle mie pre-occupazioni quotidiane, is the Italian translation of the DSES joy question (14). When we translate this sentence back into English, it reads, "During worship or at various moments when I feel in tune with God, I perceive a joyous feeling which raises me from my daily worries." The Italian language opens up this item, directing our attention to our sense of being in tune with, or harmonious with, the divine.

Love and Divine Presence as Connection

Love is a major theme in and of itself, as we explored in Chapter 6. Love does much more than connect us. But when others love me, and I love others, we connect in a powerful way. Love does connect us. Music, film, and video can remind us of this mutual connection through love, bring it home to us even when connection may seem lacking in daily life. There is a glorious music video whose music and abstract forms interacting and intermingling affirms for me our connection with each other and with a divine source: Olafur Arnald's 3055.[5] Do we engage in a pas de deux with God in our lives, directly or in relationship with others? Is there someone to take our hand, metaphorically speaking, and dance with us? And does this translate into a sense of presence, not in terms of some stiff, large statue of God, but moving life, real connection?

Love can both create and represent connection. "Ubi Caritas" is a hymn used while people wash each other's feet on Maundy

Thursday in Lent, a reenactment of Christ washing his disciples' feet.

> *Ubi caritas et amor est vera Deus ibi est.*
> Wherever love and charity are real and true, God is there.

Durufle's *Requiem* contains a beautiful musical version of this.[6] This phrase reminds me that in the moments of my day when I truly love others, and allow myself to feel their love for me, God is there. The divine is present.

God's presence often does not fit into our preconceived ideas. A simplistic notion of God, of the divine transcendent, will often not hold up to the messiness of life. No one wants to be in a relationship with an ogre in the sky, to actively seek the presence of such a being. Our images of God shape our openness to being in God's presence. Is God full of love and mercy and yet a being that appreciates beauty, truth, and justice? A God with values in some wider way, with integrity, with principles. Deep analysis belongs in religious and theological texts, which this is not. But our notion of God—or the divine as present in our lives, however we envision the divine—needs to be broad and deep enough in scope to encompass the holy, the eternal. This is important to our sense of spiritual connection.

We do not want to be accompanied on life's journey by a make-believe God. We want reality. How do we stay open to a "more than" concept of divine presence? Can we feel God's presence without pinning God down like a butterfly pinned to a board? Christian theologians have struggled for centuries to describe the trinitarian notion of God—God as creator of the universe, person full of humanity, and spirit within us, all at once. I am glad I don't have to explain that to a young child! If God is simple, it is a simplicity that unfolds into ultimate complexity.

I like to be with those who want to be with me. So this connection with God in daily life may require us to realize some sort of invitation on God's part—God, the divine, the holy, actually desiring to be with us. An invitation, such as a loving grandmother or grandfather might offer. Many feel the presence of the divine in times of conscious prayer or at other times set aside from the flurry of the day. Vulnerability and honesty are required. We need to be willing to be ourselves. We also have to be radically open, to allow God to be fully God.

Many religious traditions call for setting aside time with God, but there are also ways to become more aware of the presence of the divine in the midst of the day's mundane tasks. In the seventeenth century, Lawrence, a former soldier, entered a Carmelite monastery as a lay brother, where he became much loved for his friendliness and devotion. A little book of his letters to others, called *The Practice of the Presence of God*, describes how everything he did during the day was a way into the divine presence. He did not devote hours to silent prayer. Washing the dishes and doing the laundry became for him an opportunity for connection with the divine. I love to draw, and when I am lost in the experience of capturing the natural world with pen and ink, I often have this kind of experience. I lose track of time as a *tick, tick, tick*, and connect with a sense of eternity.

Billy Collins has a great poem called "Shoveling Snow with the Buddha," which describes enjoyment of the presence of the divine in a lighthearted way.[7] The Buddha joins silently with the poet as he shovels his driveway and, after going inside together, the Buddha suggests that they sit together and play cards. The divine and the mundane intertwined.

This congenial image of being with the divine challenges our images of God in an intriguing way. Can you think of being with the divine in this way? Does this fit with your sense of the divine? Does this provoke a reaction in you? Can you imagine shoveling snow with God? If so, what do you think that would be like? If you can't imagine doing that, why not?

Invitation to write . . .

....

....

....

....

....

....

Longing and Desire

"Be present with your want of a Deity, and you shall be present with the Deity," wrote the seventeenth-century poet Thomas Traherne. In desiring to be close to God, or in union with the divine, our passion, yearning, and longing can feed us in good ways. Detachment is all well and good, but somehow our guts yearn for direct connection. We can have an existential sense that we are not completely at home. Forcing the issue just doesn't work. Research using the DSES has found that this longing exists across the religious spectrum. Those who are deeply religious—for example, ministers in churches—can still find themselves longing for God, wanting to be closer, as evidenced in their response to the DSES question on longing (5), as well as in other ways. Those who are totally fed up with religious organizations and discouraged religiously often report feeling this, too.

This might be the time to reflect more on feelings of alienation and isolation—that is, lack of connection. We often use distractions and substances of various kinds to numb ourselves or create feelings of connection that are somehow not connected to reality. We do this to help deal with the feeling of not belonging or aloneness or meaninglessness. However, I continue to learn that a certain degree of longing and an uncomfortable sense of separation are not something to struggle against, but valid elements of the spiritual life. In an interview, the writer Henri Nouwen commented that it is sometimes in the midst of the loneliness and feelings of isolation in our social lives that we particularly find a space for connection with the divine.[8]

Write about any feelings of alienation you might have. Also describe your desires, your deep longings. How do you go about satisfying your need for connection and addressing any pains of alienation? Do you sometimes feel lonely and/or feel like you do not belong? What do you do at these times? Do you ever feel a longing for greater connection with God or the transcendent "more than"? How does this relate to these other feelings?

Invitation to write . . .

If you find yourself scoring low on the many connection questions in the DSES (especially 1, 2, 3, 12, 13, and 14), just answering the questions, writing about your experiences, and sharing with others can help you find hidden connections in life. The poetry, music, and thematic and artistic suggestions throughout this book can help, too.

How Close?

Seyyed Hossein Nasr, a renowned Muslim scholar, said in a speech in 2008,

> Moreover, for us God is the Creator and Sustainer of the universe, at once Transcendent and Immanent. . . . Over the many centuries of our history, men and women of our two communities [Christian and Islam] have stood in awe before the majesty of God as Transcendent and felt His closeness as the Immanent, for as the Noble Quran asserts: God is closer to us than our jugular vein.[9]

The circumstances of our lives, past and present, affect our ability to feel close to God as well as other people. We may not trust anyone—God included! On the other hand, some who have had horrendous experiences as children can still form close relationships. Our temperament also affects how easily we become close to others—intimacy is easier for some of us. Our religious background may encourage or get in the way of this closeness. We may have a concept of the divine as distant and untouchable, or we may just not want to be close to a being described in an unlikable way. But taking all this into account, there is some capacity in all of us for connection with the divine in a way that has power to buffer our loneliness and address some deep desires.

A hot area of psychology is "attachment theory." Much psychology research shows that having a secure sense of "attachment" helps us to form better relationships with others. One way we get this secure attachment is by growing up with a loving parent or similar person in our lives. Research has shown that another way to enhance this sense of secure attachment is to call God to mind.[10] This can be a way to remind ourselves that we have a "secure" attachment, which, in turn, frees us up to relate to others in a less needy fashion, leading to more healthy relationships. Based on this research, we can see that a keen perception of the presence of God in our lives can enhance other aspects of life, especially as we relate to others.

Our connections with other people are so important in our lives. However, connections with other people change. Our romantic relationships may dissolve, we may have irreconcilable differences with family members, we may lose our jobs and those professional relationships sustained by our professional identity. Loved ones die. Throughout all these changes, however, the transcendent connection remains—in the details, but more than in the details. The sense of closeness with the divine can be a touchstone to return to in the midst of change.

Patrick Kavanagh describes some of that in his poem "The One":

> Green, blue, yellow and red—
> God is down in the swamps and marshes,
> Sensational as April and almost as incred-
>   ible the flowering of our catharsis.
> A humble scene in a backward place
> Where no one important ever looked;
> The raving flowers looked up in the face

Of the One and the Endless, the Mind that has baulked
The profoundest of mortals. A primrose, a violet,
A violent wild iris—but mostly anonymous performers,
Yet an important occasion as the Muse at her toilet
Prepared to inform the local farmers
That beautiful, beautiful, beautiful God
Was breathing His love by a cut-away bog.[11]

The theme of connection may be expressed in your life in many ways—connections with other people, those who are like you, and those who are very different; connections with eternity, the natural world, with all of life; the flow of love; connections with the divine transcendent; feelings of alienation and desire for transcendent connection.

If this theme of connection is particularly important to you, and you want to follow it in a daily way, you can use the total DSES numerical score to do this, as all the items address connection in one way or another, even though some do this more explicitly than others. Reflect on when you feel connection to all of life in the natural world (3). Or when you feel God's love directly or through others, when you experience connection (6 or 7). Or when you accept others even when they do things you think are wrong and you establish a common bond (9).

Another way to use the DSES questions to increase your ability to see connections in your life is to go through each of the items, and in your writing focus on the experience of transcendent connection in particular as you describe your daily experiences.

8 Yes!

Hope is not the conviction that something will turn
out well, but the certainty that something makes sense,
regardless of how it turns out.
—Vaclav Havel, Czech president and playwright

Life is messy. I find myself wanting to be somewhere else,
be someone else. But my particular life, my particular personality, is what I have. And that's good! Not that I can't
actively make some changes and shape some results. I do some
of that. But in the midst of it all, this life is where I am, and I am
who I am.

"Now" is messy, but each moment—me, here, now—is, in its
own way, exactly right.

So many things push us away from being fully in each moment.
Advertisements present us with a shiny life we are supposed to
aspire to, encouraging us to inhabit the future. The future ends
up being more vivid than the present. Yet the present moment is
where we are and where we act, where we can affirm our lives or
deny them.

And you? Where are you? Think of a map with the "You are
here" mark. Each of us is in the midst of a wild life. It can sometimes seem like we are holding a tiger by the tail. Fundamental
acceptance of where you are in life right now can give you a peaceful place to start from and a very practical one, too—a secure foot-
ing to take the next step.

In the story "The Finest Music," from a collection of Celtic legends collected by James Stephens,[1] a group of men are debating about what the finest music in the world is. Some suggest that it is laughter, one suggests birdsong, one the ring of a spear on a shield, one the whisper of one who is moved, and so on. When the chief, Fionn, is finally asked, he says it is "the music of what happens."

Something about this story brings tears to my eyes. The finest music in the world is happening all around me—and I miss it! Egad! Life does not seem perfect, it does not seem ideal. But in the midst of it all, in the midst of the messiness and troubles, we can look for beauty, light, eternity. And sense a smile surfacing from deep within.

The DSES questions you might expect to be particularly representative of this theme are deep inner peace (16), being thankful for your blessings (15), accepting others (9), and being spiritually touched by the beauty of creation (1), but this theme may also be reflected in the frequency of other items in less direct but still potent ways, such as the connection to all of life question (3). General feelings of connection to, closeness with, and support from the divine can all contribute to this. You may benefit from returning to your written answers to these questions to find specific times and ways that you say yes. It may be useful to revisit these questions with this theme in mind. Or if this is something you would like to follow over time, you could pay specific attention to how often you experience these items in your life, and watch how your responses change over time as you pay attention to this.

We Cannot See the Future

Something may not seem to be working out in the short run but may lead to all sorts of marvelous outcomes, some of which we will never see ourselves. I want a sense that things are good, right,

OK. I look at my life and I find myself wondering, What is going on here? I want things to be smooth, I want to know what is coming down the pike. But none of us can see the future.

The Indian Jesuit teacher and writer Anthony de Mello tells an old Chinese story. A farmer's old horse is needed for his farm, but escapes into the hills. The neighbors all sympathize with him about his bad fortune, but the farmer replies, "Bad luck? Good luck? Who knows?" Then when his son is trying to tame one of the wild horses to replace the one that escaped, the son falls and breaks his leg. Again the neighbors express sympathy about his bad luck, but he says again, "Good luck? Bad luck? Who knows?" A few weeks later the army comes to the village and conscripts all the able-bodied youth, but not the farmer's son because of his broken leg. De Mello asks, Good luck? Bad luck? Who knows?[2]

Saying yes to life is not the same as blind optimism, or a smile plastered over the top of everything. It is seeing the world in a larger context. Einstein said that the most important question is, "Is the universe friendly?" Of course, awful things happen; can we still say yes to life, going forward fully alive? A researcher on the DSES sent me a cartoon showing two creatures squashed in a glass filled with water. One has his head up, the other is facing down. The one can breathe, the other can't, yet they are in the same glass. It is often our orientation to the situation that is the problem.

Reflect on one or two unpleasant events in your life. Can you see any way that they might end up being for the best in the big picture? Can you think of any good that might come of them?

Sometimes we don't see any way good can come from bad. But we just do not know what the future has in store. Can you relax into the mystery of the unknown?

What helps you to "keep your head out of the water?"

Invitation to write . . .

....

....

....

....

....

....

Yes to the Past

Saying yes to your life is not only about the present circumstances. I know that I can be sucked into regrets about the past, and they can drag down daily life. Many say that "mindfulness," living in the present moment, provides the best way to approach the world. I think mindfulness is a good idea. We do not give adequate attention to the present as it unfolds. But the past colors our present and shapes how we see the world—so coming to terms with the past is also an important part of saying yes to life now. Dag Hammarskjöld, former secretary-general of the United Nations, wrote,

> For all that has been, thank you.
> For all that is to come, yes.

The artist Richard Tipping makes humorous "road signs," which were exhibited at the Tate Modern Museum in London. One of them reads, "Wrong Day—Go Back." Sometimes it feels like that. But we did not take a turn somewhere that has led us to the wrong day.

I saw reruns of a television series from the 1990s called *Journeyman*. When the hero, a newspaper reporter, goes back in time he changes some things in the past that made life better in the future in many ways. He is also tempted to "correct" other things, like the death of someone in an accident. But when he returns to the future, he can see how the things he thought would be good to change would have caused serious problems down the line, affecting the course of relationships and history in major negative ways. We do not have a bird's-eye view of time. From our point of view, we see things that look awful. But to change those could mean other things would have to change, too. And that might not be so great. It is often beyond our imagination to see the unfolding of the world if we "just changed this one thing."

Reflect on a few events in your past that seemed bad at the time. Can you think of any good things that have resulted from them? Were some good things buried in hardship or suffering? Are there good things you would have missed out on if the unpleasant things had not happened?

Invitation to write . . .

When we say yes to the past and yes to our present circumstances, and we look toward the future with hope in the context of a greater meaning, we are seeing eternity present now.

Think back to last year, or even further back. Think of a few bless-ings. Take a few moments to reflect on them.

Invitation to write . . .

....

....

....

....

....

....

....

Rewind: Scour the Past Day for Blessings

You may also like to try the *examen* exercise that we discussed earlier. First, take some time to relax, become quiet, just breathe. Observe yesterday in your mind's eye, slowly, from beginning to end. Look at yesterday closely as if you were rerunning a video taken from your own perspective. Pay attention to the events of the day in light of looking for blessings, things that you might have appreciated but missed somehow.

Did you discover any blessings that you missed at the time? Were there things you appreciated more when you did this exercise? Write down some of this experience. What was it like?

Invitation to write . . .

....

....

....

....

....

....

Happiness

Happiness can be defined in so many ways. Some definitions are trite or fluffy. Some definitions are deep and satisfying. Philosophers such as Aristotle have defined happiness, or *eudaimonia*, as "activity in accordance with excellence," and have seen it as the highest human good. Entire scientific journals are devoted to research on happiness. Everybody seems to want it. But defining it is not easy. There are questionnaires that try to assess happiness. For example, people are asked, "How happy are you?" They respond on a scale of "As happy as I can possibly be" to "Very unhappy." We all want to be happy, but it is elusive to measure. You can be flourishing as a person, and contributing to the flourishing of the people you relate to, without smiling or being jolly. You can be deeply satisfied with life even if your life circumstances are awful. So judging yourself, your life, on the basis of a more superficial kind of happiness is probably not the best criterion.

Geneen Roth wrote in *Women, Food, and God,* "I've been miserable standing in a field of a thousand sunflowers in southern France in mid-June. . . . And I've been happy sitting with my dying

father. Happy being a switchboard operator." For an Irish Raidió
Teilifís Éireann radio documentary in 1981, a variety of people
were interviewed about what makes them happy. They shared
things as diverse as being around children, performing music
in front of small groups, and even when they thought they were
dying. As you read about research on happiness, it is important
to consider the different definitions used.[3] The social scientist
Phillip Brickman[4] compared people winning the lottery with a
group of matched controls and found that the lottery winners
were not any happier a few years later, compared with the control
group, and took significantly less pleasure from a series of mundane events. Studies have shown that the small positive events in
the day, rather than the presence of negative feelings, end up predicting how we feel about our days, looking back on them.[5] Your
Daily Spiritual Experiences can be some of those small positive
events. Happiness is complicated.

I met Vaclav Havel once, in the corridors of the Library of Congress. The encounter encouraged me to read more of his writings.
The quote on hope at the beginning of this chapter exemplifies his
positive yet pragmatic stance as president of the Czech Republic
following its release from Russian control—hope as the certainty
that things make sense, no matter how they look on the surface.

I remember my youngest daughter saying about herself, at age
twelve, "My life is perfect." I was amazed. I could see all sorts of
things about the world around her, her life, especially things I felt
responsible for, that I would have changed to improve her life. To
hear her comment was liberating for me as a mother. It let me off
the hook in a lovely way, and made me see things differently.

Evelyn Underhill, a very practical writer on the spiritual life in
the early twentieth century, wrote,

With this widening of the horizon, our personal ups and downs, desires, cravings, efforts, are seen in scale; as small and transitory spiritual facts, within a vast, abiding spiritual world, and lit by a steady spiritual light. And at once a new coherence comes into our existence, a new tranquillity and release. Like a chalet in the Alps, that homely existence gains atmosphere, dignity, significance from the greatness of the sky above it and the background of the everlasting hills.[6]

Reflect on your notion of happiness. Does everything have to be perfect at a superficial level for you to be happy? Have you ever been happy in the midst of times that might be described from the outside as being full of problems or that seemed less than ideal in many ways? Reflect on how happiness may have been there for you in these situations.

Invitation to write . . .

Irritations, Frustrations, and Distress

Sometimes the daily grind seriously gets in the way of saying yes. We want to do things, and it doesn't work out, or things do not go as quickly as we would like. An aging body or illness gets in the way of doing things we want to do. G. K. Chesterton said in his essay "On Running after One's Hat," "An adventure is only an inconvenience rightly considered. An inconvenience is only an adventure wrongly considered." It is not so much the irritating events that happen, as how we view them and weigh our feelings when the moment of irritation comes. Do we get dragged along by irritation, or do we take a wider or more humorous view? When my computer gives me grief, I do not automatically have that wonderful an approach to life, but I can definitely see where I could use this attitude. Many of the experiences in the DSES can provide me with the fuel for this. And it is not just the minor irritations, like getting a head cold at an inconvenient time. More serious and traumatic things happen to us, too, and these challenge our ability to say yes even more.

The psychologist William James wrote,

> "I accept the universe" is reported to have been a favorite utterance of our New England transcendentalist, Margaret Fuller; and when someone repeated this phrase to Thomas Carlyle, his sardonic comment is said to have been: "Gad! she'd better!" At bottom the whole concern of both morality and religion is with the manner of our acceptance of the universe. Do we accept it only in part and grudgingly, or heartily and altogether? Shall our protests against certain things in it be radical and unforgiving, or shall we think that, even with evil, there are ways

of living that must lead to good? If we accept the whole, shall we do so as if stunned into submission—as Carlyle would have us—"Gad! we'd better!"—or shall we do so with enthusiastic assent?[7]

What James describes here is not a jolly, rose-colored-glasses approach that denies that bad things happen, and that they cause us pain and distress. Rather, he is saying that a change of framing can affect how we feel when these things happen. In a book I coedited on measuring stress, we noted that a crucial part of the stress response is how we interpret events that happen in our lives—that is, what they mean to us. An area of study in psychology looks at "post-traumatic growth." Some of the studies in Chapter 5 linked more frequent Daily Spiritual Experiences with greater resiliency and more post-traumatic growth. Post-traumatic growth extends beyond resiliency. Some people not only bounce back from bad circumstances, but actually grow in all sorts of ways. Eventually, all of us will encounter difficulties ranging from minor to major. The resources represented in many of the DSES questions can help us be more resilient and grow through challenge in the midst of traumas.

It is important to restate that bad things do happen. People suffer. Things hurt. We are talking here about our overall approach to life, how we react to "the slings and arrows of outrageous fortune," rather than denying our pain, or the pain of others.

You Are Who You Are

A vital part of saying yes is being who you are.

What kind of person are you? Even if you might want to change some things about you, can you "accept *yourself* even though you do things you think are wrong"? Not accepting yourself may create a barrier to accepting others. It can stop love from flowing in your life and get in the way of expressing who you are in vital ways.

Being willing to be who you are is important for so many things. To be loved, you need to be in your own shoes, to be there. To be in a good relationship with someone else, you need to be wearing *your* shoes, not pretending to be someone else. "No truth, no relationship," said a wise friend. If I am not who I am, there is no way that I can genuinely connect with another.

Are you content with who you are, even if you see things you would like to change? Can you be merciful with yourself, when you think things that you do are wrong or when you make mistakes? Can you cheer yourself on in the tough times and applaud your successes?

List some of the good things about the kind of person you are.

Invitation to write . . .

....

....

....

....

....

....

....

Balance between Accepting and Engaging

For me, in each moment of each day there are two buttons, two options: (1) Escape and avoid, and (2) Say yes. When I say yes, to each moment, I breathe out.

Saying yes to what is going on now—to who you are, limits and all—enables you to make a difference in active ways that build on deeper ground. You are the person you are, in the situation you are in, and this is good. Escape means being less alive.

I watched a talk and performance by Evelyn Glennie, the deaf percussionist. She demonstrated how, when we are loose while playing the marimba, the tone is flowing, and when we tighten up, it takes more energy and does not sound as good. Accepting who we are and the situation we are in allows for that loosening up that enables us to create beautiful music.

When the actress Whoopi Goldberg was asked, "What has been the most spiritual experience of your life?" she said, "Really coming to terms with the fact that there are things in the world that you can't control, fix, or stop."

This is not passivity, but an attitude informed by "All will be well." We can actively say a participative yes to life. Can we say yes even when we just do not understand? We can still act, make a difference. We are potent. It's just that we can't control it all. Life is life, with its joys and sorrows and richness. It is what it is. It is not easy to balance my desires and aspirations for myself and the world with acceptance of how I am and how others are. A friend once said that I am a "make it happen" kind of person. That has its upside for sure, but I also need to be OK with things as they are, with me as I am, with people as they are, so I can step out from that solid, quiet place of acceptance.

Wendell Berry's poem "A Spiritual Journey"[8] tells of how we are on a world-discovering journey, not of miles but inches. For him, the goal is to understand, with humility and joy, that where we are right now is home.

9 Translating "God"

The whole universe consists of a symphony of strings,
and the "mind of God," about which Einstein wrote
so eloquently, is cosmic music resonating through
10- and 11-dimensional hyperspace.
—MICHIO KAKU, PHYSICIST

Pinning down your concept of the divine, as you interpret the individual questions in your daily life, and as you have reflected on the themes of love and connection, can be revealing. As you explore the interactions with the divine in your own life, has God, the divine, the holy, the transcendent, come into focus? Or have the "out of focus" qualities become more salient? Has your notion of the divine or holy changed or unfolded while making your way through the various exercises? Or has it stayed the same? Does the word *God* get in the way or does it help you? How did you personally handle the words *God/divine/holy* as you answered the questions?

I have worked on translations of the DSES into many languages. In a way, we each have our own personal language. Each word has a set of connotations and meanings that reflect your life experience and no one else's. We find evidence of this in daily misunderstandings with those we are close to. But there is enough in common among us so that we can communicate. The word *God* poses a real challenge in that way. I hope that if you have trouble with the word

God you have been able to "translate" it into "your language." As I helped Sui-man Ng work on the Mandarin Chinese translation of the DSES, we back-translated into English as we refined it. One of the phrases in the Chinese introduction to "substitute for the word *God* if you were uncomfortable with that word" included, "the higher power, the regulator, the truth of the universe," so that part of the introduction read,

> 以下項目中多次使用「神」這個名稱，如果你是有宗教信仰的，這名稱就是指你信仰的神。如果你並沒有宗教信仰，這「神」是泛指世界、大自然或宇宙中的更高力量、規律或道理。

It takes a while to find the right phrase in another language, so readers in a very different culture can still, as much as possible, answer the same questions. For scientific research, there is a limitation to how long the introduction to the scale can be, but for your own personal use, you can be more expansive.

Your Personal Language

Maybe in your own particular interior "language," *God* is not expressed in words, but in visual images, colors, or musical notes. When you hear the word *God* or read it in this book, are you able to "translate" it?

Searching and replacing the word *God* electronically might be useful if you are reading this text and responding in an electronic format. You could choose a replacement word or phrase that better represents the transcendent for you—higher power, divine, holy, Allah, G-d, the transcendent, the Creator—and the word processor could substitute that whenever the word *God* occurs. (If you don't have access to this technology, then you could just manually make the change.) It could be your own personal translation. As with all translations, though, you want to make sure that the meaning is not changed in the process. Those who translate the DSES into other languages usually work with me to make sure the translation of all the phrases maintains the meaning of the original; we have a lot of back and forth.

Antony Flew, a renowned philosopher who was previously an adamant atheist and who recently wrote about how he came to believe in God, mentions some of the words Einstein used for the divine:

> Einstein believed in a transcendent source of the rationality of the world that he variously called "superior mind," "illimitable superior spirit," "superior reasoning force," and "mysterious force that moves the constellations."[1]

If we substitute another word for *God*, are we measuring the same thing? It is crucial that the word represent something transcendent. I remember someone saying he worshipped the tree in his backyard, and asking if he could substitute that for *God*? One problem with this is that the tree can die or be cut down, or he may move to another house. So the tree does not remain the same for him. The word *God* is a pointer that seems to have a power; and if we divest it of all its content, the power of the word is no longer there. On the other hand, we are encouraged to divest it of the barnacles that have accumulated on it. These include things that are not intrinsically part of the concept, and which cause the word to decay for us, covering it up, obscuring it.

Ultimately, God is a mystery—our concept is fleshed out over time but never fully understood. Whatever, whoever, is divine for you needs to be beyond space and time, yet also here and now.

Alcoholics Anonymous, and other twelve-step programs for

addictions, tend to use the words *higher power* in their materials to keep them more "neutral." One thing that the twelve-step programs emphasize about the "higher power" is that you are not it! It is a relief for me not to be God. It lets me stop trying to control everything—a futile activity—and accept my imperfections more. Being perfect is not my role in the universe. The notion of a power higher than my own ego is liberating in many ways.

I was sitting recently with a group of Episcopalian women who were discussing how they addressed their prayers. "Sometimes I pray to God, sometimes Mary, sometimes Jesus," said one. "I pray to 'Abba.'" "I always pray to God as mother," said one. "I use the word *Lord*," said another, "because for me it just seems to me to cover more." "Sometimes I pray to the icon of the trinity, and am folded into that as I pray." All this variety in a small group of women from one religious denomination! Words just don't fully encompass the divine, the holy, the all-present love. Muslims have a prayer that gives ninety-nine names of God.

Theologies can be helpful as we flesh out some of the details of our vision of God. Religious scholars and mystics of various traditions over the centuries have written about God in ways that can help us interpret our experiences of connection with the divine in our lives, putting them in a larger context.

Keeping our eyes on the particulars highlighted in the various DSES questions can be helpful as we work through this ourselves. Abraham Joshua Heschel wrote,

> The art of awareness of God, the art of sensing his presence in our daily lives, cannot be learned off-hand. God's grace resounds in our lives like a staccato. Only by retaining the seemingly disconnected notes comes the ability to grasp the theme.[2]

*What thoughts have occurred to you regarding the nature of God,
the divine, the holy, as you have encountered divine language in the
questions and as you have been reading the text so far? What have
been some of your reactions?*

Invitation to write . . .

....

....

....

....

....

....

Some people may think they know exactly who God is and
exactly what their relationship is to the divine. I don't. For me,
answering the DSES questions, and thinking about my specific
experiences, helps me to define God in my life. I see God as personal, caring with a mother's love and also with the power and
vision to create and sustain the universe, a vast understanding that
stretches beyond my imaginings. I deal with apparent paradoxes
by holding things loosely. This approach may help us to better
define such challenging notions as pain and joy, good and evil,
our definitions and images of God, our impressions of others. We
may just be seeing the surface. What appears to be paradox may be
revealed as congruent, coherent. This becomes especially important in using this set of questions to communicate with others. Is
my image of God spacious? Do I react defensively when encountering a description of the divine that differs from mine? Do these

reactions ever help communicate or do they get in the way? Does my image of God help me to deal with apparent paradoxes? Some people see God as more personal, and others less so. I can share what I feel, and learn from others. How do I better understand those who relate to God as a person? How do I better understand those who find the word *God* a problem?

If You Are Still Encountering Obstacles with Divine Language

I am hoping by now that you are able to envision the word *God* as expansively complex, or beautifully simple, but for some people this word just has too many connotations, and they can't get over them. The DSES is used in settings where people state that they do not believe in God, and "translating" the word *God* to *divine* or *holy* or some other similar word usually gets at the transcendent for them. People who identify themselves as atheists can score very high on the DSES. Interestingly, as mentioned in Chapter 5, the study of the Basque region in Europe showed higher scores on the DSES for those who self-identified as atheists than for those who did not. However, sometimes the difficulties presented by the word seem insurmountable. If this is the case for you, focusing on the DSES questions that do not contain the word *God*, and following them in your life, may be one way of dealing with this.

Dividing up the items and excluding those that mention God is one option. But, especially for Chapters 10 and 11, on communication, it helps to try to make an effort to translate the God items into a language of your own over time. Some research projects have divided up the God and non-God questions, which can be useful for those who do not believe in a god. But, ultimately, all the questions hang together as a whole statistically, and this division does not prove predictive or useful for most research.

Some Creative Descriptions of the Transcendent

Ways other people have described the transcendent may prompt you to express your own thoughts, proving useful for finding common ground or seeing important differences. Defining God in the abstract can too easily lead to settling into defending territories—defining God with religious phrases that seem too pat and unreflective can alienate others. I sometimes find that I have more in common with people who call themselves agnostics than with those who profess beliefs in common with me. I wonder why this is so. Good, real relationship with the divine can sometimes grow in an environment of questioning doubt. If we have too clear and crisp a notion of God, and it is not a particularly expansive one, it can trap us in ways of thinking and acting that are not in harmony with God or in harmony with reality. Do we leave room for questions and growth? When our ideas about God are too definite, they can let us down when the rubber hits the road.

Can we find creative ways to express the transcendent that will better enable communication with others and illuminate our understanding of the "more than" in our lives? Here are a few creative thoughts for you to respond to.

Take time to write a few sentences in response to any that spark reactions in you.

··

··

··

··

- According to the French philosopher and social activist Simone Weil, "An atheist may be simply one whose faith and love are concentrated on the impersonal aspects of God." She also describes two prisoners whose cells adjoin, communicating with each other by knocking on the wall. The wall is the thing that separates them but it is also their means of communication. "It is the same with us and God. Every separation is a link."[3]
- The philosopher and theologian Thomas Aquinas reflected on whether "God" might not be more appropriately regarded as a *verb* rather than a noun.[4]
- Werner Heisenberg, the physicist who developed the Uncertainty Principle, observed, "The first gulp from the glass of natural sciences will turn you into an atheist, but at the bottom of the glass God is waiting for you."[5]
- The word *person* comes from the Greek πρόσωπο (prósopo), meaning "sounds through." I find it interesting to reflect on what or who sounds through me in my daily life, and how.
- Wendell Berry, the poet and environmental activist, writes, "When they told me, 'God is dead,' I answered, 'He goes fishing every day in the Kentucky River. I see Him often.'"[6]
- In teaching, I have used both the amazing micro world

and the vastness of astronomical images to explore the meaning of the divine. There is a video that does this in the context of a popular song, with lyrics that may resonate with you—the *Dear God* video by Monsters of Folk.[7]

- Einstein wrote, "This firm belief, a belief bound up with deep feeling, in a superior Mind that reveals itself in the world of experience, represents my conception of God."[8]

Invitation to write . . .

....

....

....

....

....

....

There is a long tradition of apophatic theology that urges that it is in knowing what God is *not* that we can best come close to God or in union with the divine. This is often associated with philosophies and Eastern religions, but the Abrahamic faiths have also used this means of dispelling misconceptions about God and to reinforce how any rational/analytic description of God will fall short. This approach has been used by Hindus, Buddhists, Taoists, Jews, and Muslims, and by Christians from traditions stretching from Catholic to Orthodox to Calvinist. The language of poetry can also be very helpful. You might want to make your own list of what "God is not. . . ." On the other hand, even though the divine is ineffable, words sometimes help remind us of qualities of the divine once we have removed the barnacles of dead language. One way of prayer in the Muslim tradition is to make a list of the divine attributes, qualities of the divine, and prayerfully reflect on them. This may be helpful to you. Go through the full set of sixteen questions and reflect on the qualities of the divine as you experience them. Return to the freshness of your experience.

Take a few minutes to make some notes or write in your journal.

Invitation to write . . .

....

....

....

....

....

....

Is the way you envision the divine full of peace and love, yet capable of wildness? Is there room for both immensity and intimacy in your Daily Spiritual Experiences? In the next chapter we will explore ways you might connect with others by sharing experiences. If you listen to the experiences of others, you might find yourself fleshing out your notion of the nature of the divine in your life. And your experiences of the transcendent in daily life may enable others to enrich their vision.

Part Five
Springboard for Communication

10 Why and How to Communicate Using Daily Spiritual Experiences

It is very hard to say the exact truth, even about your own
immediate feelings—much harder than to say something
fine about them which is not the exact truth.
—GEORGE ELIOT

The Daily Spiritual Experiences are personal, subtle, and yet important to us. If we knew more about each other's spiritual lives, we would also know more about what each of us values on a deeper level. This is important in committed relationships, family dynamics, therapeutic and pastoral relationships, and workplace settings.

There was a recent spate of conversations on the Web based on the question, WDYDWYD? (Why do you do what you do?) These conversations assume that if we articulate our motivations and share them, it will help us to understand ourselves and others better. This approach has been used in business settings and in social networking venues to enhance self-reflection and understanding. But we are notoriously bad at identifying the causes of our actions. For example, voting for incumbents goes up when the home sports teams are winning, and the music in stores can influence our purchasing.[1] Yet I am sure you or I would not see any role for the outcome of sporting events in our own voting behavior, or any role of background music playing in our purchasing decisions. We can, however, try to be aware of our feelings and the flavors of daily life. The DSES can increase awareness of those feelings, help us unpack them, and in the process, help us to convey them to others. The sixteen questions, when combined with the introduction to the scale and enhanced by reflection on the themes, give us simple words and number scores that enable us to find common ground with others.

We Cannot Deny the Experiences of Others, and They Cannot Deny Ours

We cannot deny the experience of others. We can question their interpretation, and challenge them to express it more clearly in language that makes sense to us, but ultimately they have had a feeling or experience and we cannot deny that. In psychological counseling and social work, especially when doing family therapy, counselors teach people to take the feelings of others at face value, and then move on, perhaps to explore their feelings or their response to the behaviors of others. For example, "I can hear that you feel angry, but I am upset that you just hit me!" It is not a good or valid tactic to tell people they should not feel angry, that feeling angry is wrong. In the same way, sharing with others about responses to the items in the Daily Spiritual Experience Scale opens the way to communicating important things at a basic level. We may have different beliefs about the structure of the universe, but that does not keep us from sharing our experiences and feelings respectfully with each other.

Specifics Can Reveal What We Have in Common

Recently, a video titled "Stuck in a Bad Project" went viral on YouTube. It was a parody of a popular song by Lady Gaga called "Bad

Romance." The video was created in their spare time by members of a science research lab in China, the Zheng Lab—with music, dancing, and costumes made of lab materials. It has been appreciated by those who have never worked in a lab, never visited China, and don't know who Lady Gaga is. Many, many people could relate to the notion of being stuck in a bad project of any kind. The particulars of the situation let us see what we have in common. When people share their stories, their particulars, we see details that help us to see our own life more clearly. In this way, keeping the discussions of spirituality focused on the sixteen questions and people's experiences, and sharing how they affect our lives, keeps things grounded. Concrete. I wrote awful poetry as an adolescent—it was full of generalities. The best poetry is specific. It shows rather than teaches. We can "show" others our experiences as we describe them with specifics.

A Chance to Inspire One Another

William James, the founder of the modern-day field of psychology who was very interested in religious experience, wrote,

> The study of the mystics, the keeping company however humbly with their minds, brings with it as music or poetry does—but in a far greater degree—a strange exhilaration, as if we were brought near to some mighty source of Being, were at last on the verge of the secret which all seek. The symbols displayed, the actual words employed, when we analyze them, are not enough to account for such effect. It is rather that these messages from the waking transcendental self of another, stir our own deeper selves in their sleep.[2]

There is something mystical in the *ordinary* sense of the word in the DSES questions. These words of James can apply to hearing others describe their ordinary spiritual experiences. Their comments can awaken something in us, too. It is easy to try to outdo one another with the spectacular nature of spiritual experience, "Mystical" with a capital *M*. But when it comes down to it, our ordinary journey might be most inspiring to others over the long haul. The little bursts of brilliance in daily life encourage others to look for similar experiences in their lives, reminding them that color is there after all.

Deep Communication Is Useful

Why bother to communicate about these kinds of things? Why not just talk about sports, the weather, shoes, various activities? I usually find it more satisfying to discuss important things, but some people don't. Some very interesting research on "disclosure" shows that sharing details and feelings about things that are important to us can be useful in a variety of ways. That's probably one of the reasons therapy works. And disclosure about spiritual issues seems to have particular power. A study by Dr. Gina Brelsford and others looked at Daily Spiritual Experiences and "spiritual disclosure," talking about spiritual issues with someone else.[3] In a large sample of adults, the researchers found that disclosure about spiritual things was linked to a concept called "generativity." Generativity includes things like the capacity to give to others and the ability to flourish in ways that have a positive effect on those around us. Brelsford states, "It may be that incorporating the sacred into conversations increases connections that people feel between themselves and society."

Even apart from this, deep communication gets at who we are.

What really drives the bus for each of us is complicated. These experiences are a way in.

The DSES Can Lead to Deeper Communication

The sixteen questions started with conversations with many kinds of people, and have proven useful in many cultures and with people with various beliefs. So when we share our experiences, and hear about those of others, we build on that body of scientific research. Conversations can also start with the themes in Part Four, "Themes," using the individual questions to focus on themes in our lives and those of others. Discussing the "Flow of Love," Chapter 6, and "Connection versus Alienation," Chapter 7, can bring relationships to life. "Translating God," Chapter 9, can help to bridge some religious issues, as long as we focus on our experience and don't use abstractions to beat others over the head! We can share with each other about our responses to the challenges of daily life using the issues in Chapter 8, "Yes!" finding undiscovered depths in others and ourselves in the process.

Translating Experience

The discussions I have with others when working on translations lead to great conversations. As we work together on them, we end up discussing important distinctions that add to my appreciation of the richness and complexity of spiritual experience. For me, this process confirms the reality of the "underlying construct"—the reality of these spiritual experiences reflected in the language. Each of us "translates" each item differently. What *selfless caring for others* (8) means to one person may be different from what it means to another. Exploring the common ground and the variations is part of the fun. English is my native language, but some other languages capture nuances of meaning that English cannot. The German and Dutch word for "caring," *sorgen*, carries connotations of worry, but in other languages that is not the case. Remember the richness of the Italian translation of question 14. Our own individual "translations" are going to be colored by our experience, our culture, and our religion. This makes for a rich conversation.

Rules of the Game

When we work in groups, ground rules are essential. Just imagine a sports game with only suggested guidelines rather than rules! ("Try to get the ball into the goal, but if you miss, and it's close, it will still count.") Another advantage of rules is that you can point to me as the bad guy, which can save face and decrease group disagreements. (Studies have shown that a common enemy increases group cohesiveness.) Remember the advice never to discuss religion and politics if you want to get along? Hopefully, these rules will help you to avoid some of the problems that might arise in the midst of sharing spiritual experience. I will try to keep these rules to a minimum. They should help to make your conversations both fun and useful. Here are ground rules I have successfully used in classes and groups over the years, followed by some detailed elaboration of each of them.

1. Respect others and expect respect in return.
2. Be specific and concrete. Resist generalities.
3. Hold things loosely.
4. Do not give unsolicited advice.
5. Do not proselytize.
6. Do not give the high ground to the dramatic.

Respect

Respect is crucial. This means valuing others even if we don't understand them. It helps to remember that we cannot deny the experience of the other person. It's not easy to adhere to this rule. Respect requires valuing others, even when we think they are totally wrong! But it's a two-way street: if we want respect, we need to give it. And don't forget to respect yourself if you are one of those people who tend to devalue your own opinions.

Another aspect of respect is respecting the rights of others to their silence. I remember being in a group expertly led by Parker Palmer, a writer and leader of workshops in the areas of leadership and education. He remarked that this was not a "share or die" environment. If people choose not to share, respect their right to silence.

Be Concrete Rather Than Abstract

Resist generalities. Return to the concreteness of your own experiences. Take one question at a time, one theme at a time. Give it its full due.

I have spent a lot of unpleasant times in strategic planning discussions in organizational settings. When people drifted away from the particulars, the discussion tended to become ineffective. The words may have sounded good, but they signified little. We live our lives in the particulars, and the DSES questions build on particular experiences. Through particulars, we build connections with one another. Abstractions are comfortable, but in this case, they get in the way. When you feel the conversation floating up into the abstract ether, or into theologically pat phrases, pull your comments and those of others back down to particular real-life experiences. Go back to the specific times that you "counted" when you were answering the questions in Chapter 3. Talk about them, and how they felt to you.

For many of us, it is so much easier to talk in "oughts" but it is *you* I want to get to know, not some abstract understanding of an ideal. There is vulnerability in specifics. Look back on the specifics that others shared with me and that I shared with you in Chapter 3, where you had a chance to express your experiences: The woman who looked to God to support her as she returned home on the bus, tired after work. My struggles with deep inner peace in the midst of a caffeinated personality. The person who felt God's presence during the birth of her baby. There is a safety in generalities that we tend to drift to, and this is one of the reasons theologies, useful though they may be, can let us down and fail to touch our hearts.

I share my life, you share your life, and then we can appreciate the richness in each of us.

Hold Things Loosely

Words are inadequate, and misunderstandings are a fact of life. When I laugh at myself it helps. The humorist Dave Barry does such a good job of highlighting our differences with humor, and especially noticing the foibles of guys, from a guy point of view. For example, "If a woman has to choose between catching a fly ball and saving an infant, she actually makes the choice to save the infant without considering if there is a man on first base." Sometimes it is easier for us to see the humor in others, but there are jokes that remind us of our own foibles, and it feels good to laugh about them. You could probably reflect on your own beliefs and actions and find similar incongruities.

Holding things lightly doesn't mean you minimize your own

passions. We all come from a specific place—our family background, the religious tradition of our social group, our own religious beliefs, doubts and reactions, personal beliefs. Denying what has shaped us religiously, culturally, and psychologically, and trading it for smiling mush, just does not work. This paradoxical stance of passion and openness can lead to great conversations with others.

Among the things we need to hold loosely are pain and joy, our definitions of many things, our images of God, our impressions of others. We may just see the surface. As we laugh, we break open our shell. In the process what appears to be paradox may be revealed as more congruent, coherent.

Listen Rather Than Advise

It feels great to give people advice. Often, we're formulating the advice as people are talking, which gets in the way of hearing what they're saying. You know how great it is to feel that someone is listening to you. I once had a conversation over dinner with the television journalist Bill Moyers. He was not interviewing me, but I had the sense that he was hanging on my every word. I am sure that is one reason he makes such a good interviewer, one who is able to draw people out of themselves.

The value of our advice is limited by our inadequate understanding of other people's experience. We have not walked a mile in their shoes. Even when we are invited to advise, our advice falls short. We need to keep this in the front of our minds. I remember the cover image on a children's book by Babette Coles, *I Am Not You*. The cover art pictured a dad standing in front of a mirror, and the mirror image showed him in a ballerina costume. I am not you. You are not me. It really helps to remember that.

There was a great retro 1950s image on a refrigerator magnet of a woman taking a pie out of the oven, and saying to the woman next to her, "I don't recall asking for your advice." The best conversations using the DSES questions involve listening. It is amazing what we hear when we listen.

No Proselytizing

These conversations are not the place to try to convince others that your set of beliefs, or your personal or political stance, is the true one.

Polish poet Czeslaw Milosz wrote,

> When someone is honestly 55% right, that's very good and there's no use wrangling. And if someone is 60% right, it's wonderful, it's great luck, and let him thank God. But what's to be said about 75% right? Wise people say this is suspicious. Well, and what about 100% right? Whoever says he's 100% right is a fanatic, a thug, and the worst kind of rascal.[4]

This is not to say that we cannot be passionate about our faith or personal stance. This passion can add to our conversation, making it vibrant. These are things we care about, after all. But it is all too easy to slip from strong personal convictions to proselytizing and conflict, especially if we are feeling threatened by disagreements.

It is a spiritual discipline to maintain passion and roots in our own faith, while having a radical openness to other people, their ways of seeing the world, and their intrinsic value. You may find other places where constructive dialogue about beliefs is relevant, but conversations using the DSES work best when focused on the experiences and themes.

Resist Giving the High Ground to the Dramatic

These questions focus on the ordinary. (In fact, sometimes I wish I had used "Ordinary" rather than "Daily" in naming the scale.) There is a reason the scoring scale is frequency. We do not rank Daily Spiritual Experiences by degree of drama.

I read memoirs now and again, or hear talks. I also enjoy fiction, and a great novel or play or movie can convey truths in powerful ways. But more and more these days I hear and see people enhancing their descriptions of their lives by weaving fiction into true stories when they write "memoirs" or give talks. This makes me balk. Radical honesty in descriptions of ourselves to others is good for us and good for others. Is the ordinary not good enough for us? If so, that is too bad, since that is where we live. Another problem with the "enhanced" version of our own life stories is that it may cause others to feel less grounded and happy with their own life in comparison. If they are comparing their life to fiction, what a sorry state of affairs.

Bask in the glory of the ordinary experiences of your days.

11 Organizational, Professional, and Personal Uses

Our hearts are not stones. A stone may disintegrate in time
and lose its outward form. But hearts never disintegrate. . . .
We can always communicate them to one another.
—HARUKI MURAKAMI, NOVELIST

This book, with the sixteen DSES questions and the four themes, can enhance communication in many settings. Having looked at why sharing about experiences might be useful, and the basic rules for doing so, we turn in this chapter to some suggestions for use in particular groups, places, and settings, including

- Secular organizations and businesses
- College students, adolescents, and the young at heart
- Religious groups or faith-based organizations
- Therapeutic settings, among psychotherapists, social workers, hospice workers, addiction treatment counselors, family therapists, and chaplains; in prisons; and counseling those with chronic disease, declining function, or PTSD
- Family members, partners, friends
- Interreligious or intercultural dialogue

How best to structure communication depends on the setting. Some specific ideas include weekly discussion groups, retreats, one-on-one counseling, couples or small-teams conversations, and online discussion groups. A one-day or half-day retreat might be more appropriate for business settings, while a weekly discussion over six or even sixteen weeks, with time off in between, might be more appropriate for other groups. Some groups can be self-directed; others may work better with a leader.

Secular Organizations

Secular organizations can draw on the DSES as presented in this book in a variety of ways. The DSES has been used as a research tool for doctoral theses exploring how these ordinary experiences affect altruistic and cooperative behaviors in a business setting. One study established a connection between more frequent Daily Spiritual Experiences scores and the likelihood of pursuing a public service career.[1] Figuring out what motivates and sustains employees and volunteers is crucial as organizations try to incorporate values and ethical principles in their work. Administering the DSES can help organizations identify these factors.[2] In addition, the DSES questions enable organizations to address spiritual issues without polarizing the conversation into religious debate.

In many service organizations, burnout is a serious issue. More frequent responses to the sixteen DSES questions have been linked to less burnout among teachers, ministers, social workers, and health care providers.[3] This makes these questions particularly useful for discussion in organizations that serve others and pursue altruistic ends. Discussion of the DSES and the themes of love and connection can encourage support for one another and help to explore what keeps us enlivened. Groups of professionals who directly care for others, such as social workers, health care professionals, and those working with the dying or the bereaved, need to find sources of renewal. The capacity of the DSES to address a wide variety of cultures and faiths, plus its capacity to embrace a secular orientation, can promote deep discussion among people in these professions.

I participated in a conference called "The Love That Does Justice," sponsored by the Ford Foundation. Participants were primarily nonprofit leaders, those working in organizations trying to do good, often with meager economic resources. The flow of love theme is crucial to those operating in areas where the rewards are often low and the flack is high. Those who give of self for the good of others on a daily basis need to find ways to recharge. Exploring how Daily Spiritual Experiences might provide some of that is a worthwhile exercise. And doing it in a group can be especially valuable. Particular relationship malfunctions can happen in the nonprofit world when we depend too much on reinforcement from those we give to.

In many organizations, discussions using the DSES and its themes can highlight underlying motivations. *Immunity to Change*,[4] a great book about organizations, helps individuals in an organizational context identify often-unrecognized motivations driving their behaviors. We may want to change, but stronger personal motivations we are not aware of keep us from making the desired change. The DSES items can provide insights into motivational patterns based on our perceived relationship with the transcendent and our spiritual connections. These can fuel the kinds of changes that we wish to see in our lives and our relationships with others in a work setting. It also allows us to connect with those we work with at a deeper and more realistic level, seeing others not just as functional units, but of value in themselves. We can also see more clearly our own value grounded in something "more than," which can mitigate interpersonal conflicts and distress.

Conversations about the DSES can help identify the roots of our values. They can create a neutral space for discussion of religious/spiritual values that might fuel and influence how we work. This can be particularly helpful in times of organizational transition and ethical crisis. As we express things that are important to us and communicate with others productively about these things, we often find common ground even if our beliefs differ.

College Students, Adolescents, and the Young at Heart

Drafts of this book and the scale itself work particularly well with young people. I have used the ideas in secular college classes myself. It can open up discussion and allow young people to voice questions and work through them in a nonjudgmental way.

Within religions and faith traditions there is often a generational divide. In some ways, parents and adolescents are from different cultures. In the book *American Grace*, sociologist Robert Putnam emphasizes the growing importance of relationships and understanding between those of different religions in the American landscape. He also points out that a rising number of young people find so many problems in religious organizations that they are withdrawing from religion altogether or pursuing a spiritual path apart from any religious group. The DSES includes items that address those who think of themselves as "spiritual but not religious" as well as those whose roots are religious, and it can offer a chance for much-needed communication between the two groups.

You need to learn to listen.
—EVELYN GLENNIE, SCOTTISH DEAF DRUMMER

A recent study used the DSES to examine young people's interest in spirituality and caring for the natural world in a very different context—surfers and scuba divers in New Zealand. Another ongoing study in Malaysia is looking at ecotourism and the spiritual, using the DSES. The scale can call up a variety of ways of connecting with the transcendent both in religious and less explicitly religious ways.

In David Foster Wallace's 2005 commencement speech at Kenyon College he said,

> There are these two young fish swimming along and they happen to meet an older fish swimming the other way, who nods at them and says, "Morning, boys. How's the water?" And the two young fish swim on for a bit, and then eventually one of them looks over at the other and goes, "What the hell is water?"[5]

What we assume about life is often so different from the assumptions of others. This can be especially true between generations. The DSES provides an open environment for people—young and old—to avoid pat answers on religious topics. Rather they can explore the way they experience spiritual connection and divine love in their lives, and reflect on, and share about, how that might be encouraged in creative ways.

Religious Groups and Faith-Based Organizations

The DSES questions can open dialogue within a single tradition and promote our understanding of each other, in addition to enhancing awareness of the transcendent in ourselves. While the DSES has increasingly been used as an assessment tool in religious settings and faith-based organizations, it can be even more fruitful as a tool for promoting communication, for example, in discussion groups where people explore the specifics of their spiritual lives with the DSES questions.

Approaching our concept of God with radical openness provides space for God. If we pin down the divine too much and ignore others' views, we can end up with an impoverished notion of the divine. We learn about the vastness of the divine by listening to the experiences of others. If we think of God as a judgmental autocrat, we can learn from those with a clear sense of God's loving-kindness. If our notion of God excludes the presence of the divine in the natural world, we can learn from those who see creation as imbued with the glory of God, the Creator. If our notion of God is sweet, those who see God's sense of justice may enliven our relationship with the divine. This breadth of vision can be found among many who are affiliated with the same religious organization.

Structuring a discussion group or a reading group around the DSES items and themes in the context of a synagogue, mosque, or church setting can encourage deeper discussion and connection. Participants could go through the items and themes together and share experiences and reactions, then do some of the exercises and questions in the text as a group, exploring this richness together, appreciating differences, and celebrating commonalities. Structures ranging from four to sixteen weeks can work well for this.

Administrators of explicitly religious organizations, such as faith-based hospital systems, faith-based colleges, and religious communities of various kinds, can benefit from using the DSES to increase communication. In addition, these managers can gain insight into how work and values connect with the experience of transcendent connection in daily life in a way that can be useful both to the organization and to those who work there.

Therapeutic Settings

Therapeutic professionals working with the DSES include social workers, psychologists and psychiatrists, pastoral counselors and clergy, college counselors, military chaplains, hospice workers, and prison counselors. The scale is being used in rehabilitation counseling and addiction treatment facilities, as well as with those suffering from post-traumatic stress disorder (PTSD). It is being used in residential care for abused and neglected children and adolescents, in hospice, and with those aging in the midst of declining functioning. Because the scale has scope for a variety of religious views, it can work well in therapeutic settings where the client and the professional have differing religious and spiritual outlooks. The DSES questions and themes can be particularly useful for the therapist who is actively engaged in incorporating the spiritual aspects of a person's life into solutions to problems. The scale scores can give a quick overview of clients' spiritual experience and feelings. Even more valuable, the scale can open up the conversation and uncover things about their daily life that can help the professional better care for them. It can help the professional identify aspects of clients' lives that may be particularly important to them and resources for resiliency and coping that they may be able to draw on in difficult times.

The "rules of the game," outlined in the previous chapter, are important for therapeutic relationships, too. In these relationships, the client has implicitly come to seek advice. How does your advice as a therapist fit the client's particular spiritual experiences?

In a presentation and workshop session I gave at a psychiatry conference in Romania, the questions themselves gave the psychiatrists attending the conference a way to explore their own approaches to the spiritual aspects of life. This enabled some of them to better appreciate the role of spirituality in their patients' lives, rather than seeing the spiritual language patients used as creating a gulf between them. They also realized that, without needing a common set of beliefs, using the scale could open up conversation about the kinds of resources that might help particular patients in their struggles.

Recently, I received an email from someone using the DSES as part of research for a social work doctoral thesis, examining spiritual experiences of people on dialysis with end-stage renal disease. In mentioning why she was using the scale, she said, "The scale is simple to administer and it does not inject a particular spiritual perspective, but allows the client to describe their personal spiritual experience. I also think the scale will open the door for further discussion with the client." This seems to be happening in a variety of settings.

While doing research in a hospital in Brazil, a PhD researcher administered the sixteen questions to many patients. One, an older Jewish man, said he did not want to fill out the questionnaire. He said he knew his religion and did not want to discuss this at all. He identified the researcher as not being Jewish, and he was concerned that she wanted to proselytize. But in her lovely, engaging manner, she said she understood, but that she thought he might just want to look at the questions anyway. It was the beginning of a rich conversation about faith and God and what was important to him, and to her, too. In the end, he was glad to answer the spiritual experience questions. But the more important outcome was the two-way communication that took place and the bond that formed between them. She talked with me about how much they discovered they had in common.

The DSES questions and themes can be particularly useful for the therapist who is actively engaged in incorporating the spiritual aspects of a person's life into solutions to problems—for example, chaplains, counselors who take a particularly spiritual approach, and people working in hospice.

Deepening Relationships: Increasing Connection with Family, Partners, and Friends

Points raised in the other settings can also apply to family, friends, and other close relationships. We assume things about those we are close to, categorizing them in ways that are often inaccurate. Sharing responses to the DSES and our answers to questions throughout this book can provide fresh ways to communicate about things that inform our lives, enabling us to better under-stand those close to us. Sharing these details and perspectives can contribute to getting along, and we can also help one another flourish in the process. It can help bridge intergenerational differ-ences in religious views in a respectful way. The sixteen questions are especially useful when religious differences seem to separate us. By sharing our responses to the DSES and the kinds of spiritual resources we find useful in our lives with those close to us, we can relate to them in a deeper way.

Doing self-tests and sharing the results can provide a struc-ture as we recognize our differences and commonalities. But do remember that even in informal sharing, it's essential to follow the "rules of the game." And, as mentioned in Chapter 4, baseline sensitivities may differ. So comparing total scores can be decep-tive. One person may have many of one kind of experience, but rarely many of the others. And even scores on individual items can reflect individual differences that prevent direct comparison. The most important value of the scores as described in this book is in watching our own individual personal scores change over time. Enjoy the variety.

It is particularly important in communication with those close to us to give permission not to share about certain things. Moreover, those we are close to are most likely to see the gap between how we want to be and the ways we grapple with the challenges of daily life. Extending mercy, kindness, acceptance, and sensitivity are particularly important as we listen to the Daily Spiritual Experiences and challenges of those close to us.

Interreligious, Secular-Religious, and Intercultural Dialogue

In some ways we are all from different cultures, as we have each had unique life experiences. We may share a common religious label with someone, but still have vast differences in our thinking and approach to life. On the other hand, we sometimes assume a uniformity that just does not exist. But the DSES questions, the responses in Chapter 3, and the themes in Chapters 6 through 9 can be particularly helpful when cultures and religious beliefs differ, by increasing understanding and communication, and bridging perceived divisions.

Conflict is a big problem in today's world. But this is nothing new, as students of world history know. An "us against them" mentality can be comforting. Different cultural or ethnic groups are often defined by religious labels. I lived in Northern Ireland for ten years. In my research and in my life there, I saw clearly that while the groups were labeled "Protestant" and "Catholic," the divisions were more cultural and ethnic than they were religious. I taught chemistry at the Boys' Model Secondary School, and the boys there said they could identify the Catholics because their eyes were closer together! Accents gave the tip-off regarding which "side" people were on. Religious labels were handier than "Celtic," "nationalist," "unionist," "Scottish ancestry," though these were all equally applicable labels. The level of misunderstanding that can arise in such situations spreads to the attitudes and prejudices about people's religious lives and can cut to the core of identity in serious and often detrimental ways.

The sixteen questions and the associated themes, however, offer a bridge over theological and cultural divides. In fact, the DSES has been used in two projects I know of in Northern Ireland, and it was chosen because of the scale's applicability to many and its lack of divisiveness. The capacity for this set of questions to stimulate dialogue has been shown even more widely as the instrument has been used with Muslims, Hindus, and indigenous peoples. This has also been demonstrated in Taiwan, where the Mandarin translation has been used in a population that is primarily Buddhist, but where there is a wide variety of religious beliefs.

In some ways we are all engaged in intercultural dialogue. Yes, we may have more in common with some people than others. Yet we can also have profound differences from those who seem very much like us. I was at the State of the World Forum one year, surrounded by people from many countries. I was speaking with a monk from Ireland over coffee and as we were discussing some of my work in spirituality and measurement, he said that he suspected the spiritual differences between all his fellow monks would be radical in terms of beliefs, attitudes, and experience. Then at lunchtime I shared a table with two men from Israel and Palestine who had been great friends over the years, working for peace in that region. Their friendship and respect for each other's religious stance was obvious in their conversation. So where are the cultural divides really?

Bridging these differences can bring individuals together, which in turn can have a "trickle-up" effect. There are many other resources for interreligious and intercultural conversation.[6] The DSES can add to the conversation. It gives us a way to communicate without fleeing from discussion of religious tradition altogether.

Samir Selmanovic describes his efforts to bridge the divides among those of various religions, springing from his Yugoslavian background that included Muslim, atheist, and Christian family members.[7] He quotes Yehuda Amichai, the Israeli poet: "The moles and plows of love soften the stomped soil of a hard ground where we are right." One interesting point he makes is that various religions have become "God management systems," but that God doesn't need us to do the managing. What a relief. In using the DSES in conversations with those different from us, we can leave our defensive postures at the door, and just enjoy learning from, being with, and sharing with them.

I can truly love someone, even when he has things about him that I do not like. No one is perfect. I can respect a person even if I disagree with him. This kind of deep, fundamental respect is the foundation on which communication with others rests, particularly in the area of spiritual experiences. I have a particular faith that fuels my life, and I nest that in a religious tradition. Instead of putting blinders on me, that grounding has allowed me to better learn from those of other faiths, and enjoy hearing about their experiences. I love differences, and have no desire for us all to be the same. Like a tree in autumn, the more color the more beautiful. The depth of color contributes to the beauty. It's the same with religious depth. The most illuminating conversations I have had about spirituality have been with those who were deeply committed to their particular faith tradition, be it Hindu, Muslim, Jewish, Christian. They saw the messiness of life and of their religious persuasion, but nevertheless kept on digging deeper.

I like it when people dress differently, speak a different language, eat different foods than I do. I have learned much from conversations with those from other religions and spiritual perspectives. I have also learned much from delving into the depths and history of one particular tradition and just swimming in it through the turbulence. I have benefited from developing roots. When I traveled to Greece, the food in Thessaloniki was part of a long history and cultural mélange. Yes, mixing of traditions happened, but it didn't end up being a uniform oatmeal.

There is also something invigorating about communicating with an individual who is genuinely open, still undecided about where to invest his or her religious commitment, still determined to survey the landscape first. People may have many good reasons to take this agnostic stance: A religious framework from childhood that just will not hold water; a reaction against bigotry, simplistic religious descriptions, arrogance, hypocrites, corruption; and wanting to hold out for religious connections that will not be superficial, but rather address the richness of our capacity for spiritual experience.

The list of questions in the Daily Spiritual Experience Scale can open bridging conversations. By examining particular experiences of transcendent connection and themes that underlie those, we can make connections and understand one another better. However, there is no shortcut that avoids openness and respect. Have you noticed that the most secure people are often the most able to listen to the viewpoints of others? Their quiet confidence allows you to be fully you. As you have conversations with others, you, too, can be secure in your spiritual experiences. They are real; they are yours.

In the midst of these conversations, leaving space for difference is important. There is something in the cultural and religious background of another person that is truly different from our own. I was once in a work meeting that used the external symbols of Christian Communion to create an atmosphere of reverence and connection. I came away feeling that this could well be offensive to those for whom Communion with bread and wine has a very particular meaning. Rather than bridging, it could be demeaning of a vital practice. Recently, some Hindus in the United States have been troubled by the secular appropriation of yoga in Western societies that minimizes and/or distorts the underlying religious meaning in the exercises and practice. I like doing yoga, and find the breathing and body awareness very helpful. How do I enjoy the positive contribution of yoga, while still respecting the tradition that it emerged from? A respect for theology and practices does not assume that I can easily, or possibly ever, step into the shoes of others—their culture and religious heritage. These are not issues to be dealt with lightly by mushing everything together.

Finally, when we encounter differences, and even when we see similarities, we tend to scurry into beliefs. I am not saying that beliefs are unimportant. They *are* important. But they too often can be used as clubs—in both senses of the word. First, as an in-group, a club to which you belong and the other doesn't. And second, as a club to beat the other with, with rational or irrational argument. As we explore the finer details of our own spiritual experiences, and then communicate those with others, can we connect with others in ways that avoid some of the problems of seemingly clashing beliefs? Instead of arguing about doctrine, can we focus on the real in each of our lives, as we each understand it?

Continuing the Conversation

Your explorations so far have helped you to find a language for your experiences and important themes in your life that will enable you to communicate with others in a variety of ways. You can continue the conversation even with those who have not used the questions and themes.

John Woolman was an eighteenth-century Quaker speaker and advocate for social justice in America. In his diary, there is a story of the Algonquin chief who, on hearing Woolman speaking in a language he did not understand, said, "I love to hear the place where the words come from." When I communicate with others about spiritual connection, the flow of love, our common sense of the role of connection with the divine in our lives, and our views of the world in a wider context, I want to hear the place where the words come from, and share that place with others. All of us who have used the DSES and the other tools in this book are better equipped to do that now, and I hope you are, too.

PART SIX
Awake and Alive

12 What Now? What Next?

Experience is a myriad richness. We think more than
we can say. We feel more than we can think. We live more
than we can feel. . . . And there is still much more.
—EUGENE GENDLIN, PHILOSOPHER AND PSYCHOTHERAPIST

Y ou have given your attention to the things discussed in
this book, and you have drawn your attention explicitly
to the questions and experiences in your life. You have
thought about, discussed, and/or written about them. You found
some that you have more frequently, and some that may be less
relevant. You have exposed yourself to the experiences of others,
broadening your notion of what to look for. And you have explored
some of the underlying themes that may link some of those experiences for you and others. You looked at them from a different
perspective, and, in the process, made them more available to you.

The Quality and Variety of Your Experiences

By this time in the process, if you have responded to the questions
as you have gone through the book, you will probably have already
increased your total/average number scores on the questions.
Probably not all, but some. If you're using the numbers in this
way, has this actually been the case for you? Are there any of the
individual questions that you think you would get a higher score

on now than you did the first time around? Try it out by taking the entire DSES (in the Appendix) again.

But remember that the process is not primarily about the number scores. Increasing the quality and variety of the kinds of experiences you are having also "counts" as increasing your spiritual experiences. Tracking your particular experiences in words may be your way of revisiting the questions, rather than tracking the number scores: You may wish to jot down any new experiences you have had since the first time you answered the questions, linking them to the individual questions. The numbers are crude approximations—by contrast, your specific perceptions and descriptions are rich and detailed. Changes do not always show up in the number scores, for many reasons, including those mentioned in Chapter 2. You can also go back to Chapter 3, where you considered each of the sixteen questions in detail, and look over the individual items in detail once again. If you are finding more evidence of the "more than" in particular ways, you may want to jot down additional experiences in another color ink, a different font color, or on a new page of your journal with today's date. Your descriptions are worth writing down both for your future inspiration and to inspire others.

You may have discovered a few of the questions you would like to focus on, or you may want to continue to seek more frequent experiences across the board. You may wish to circle those you would like to especially follow over time: Ones you would like more of, or ones that seem especially important to you in your daily life. If you are using the numbers, you have a total average score, you have subsets of items that also can be averaged, and you have scores on individual items of special interest to you.

I am reminded of the comment by the French author Marcel Proust: "It would even be inexact to say that I thought of those who read it, as readers of my book. Because they were not, as I saw it, my readers. More exactly they were readers of themselves, my book being a sort of magnifying glass . . . by which I could give them the means to read within themselves."[1] Hopefully this book has given you one or more magnifying glasses for "reading yourself."

Specific Ways to Fold the Questions into Your Daily Life

The more you fold the use of the questions into the habits and patterns of your days, the more of these experiences you can continue to find. Here are a variety of specific ways you can do this:

1. Take a question a week and write about it each morning or evening—just a few sentences, or more if you enjoy writing. For example, you could focus on the deep inner peace question (16), reflecting on moments when you may have experienced this in your life, even in the midst of worries. Then try to identify aspects of your life that make these moments possible.

2. Answer the full set of questions each Saturday or Sunday morning (or whatever is the least busy day in your week). Add up the total and compare it to the week before. Do not judge yourself, just look at what is happening to your score over time. Are there things that make it go up or down, as you live your life, encountering people and engaging in activities and events? Do not just look at the numbers, but give yourself space to write down a few notes on the specifics of the experiences. Reflect on what else has been going on in your week and write something about how you think your life experience may be affecting the frequency of your spiritual experiences.

3. Pick a subset of questions that you are particularly interested

in and regularly answer these questions, following your written responses over time, and/or the average score for those. For example, if you feel alienated or lonely, which of the questions do you think might especially help you to find resources that might help with these feelings?

4. Use the list of questions as a checklist that you revisit frequently. Ask yourself for each of the statements, Have I experienced this today? You could do this on a daily basis, or once every few days, and total the number of check marks each time. This can provide another tracking method that might work for you. (You might, for example, put a copy of the questions in a spreadsheet on your desktop.)

5. Take one of the themes and focus on it over time, using the questions. For example you may wish to dwell on the times in your days when you experience love flowing in, describing them when they happen and reflecting on times love may be flowing in and you missed it. Use the questions to explore the balance of love in your life over time. Is it flowing? You may wish to follow one of the other three themes in more depth. By seeing the individual questions as connected to an underlying theme, you may find that they link together coherently and have even more positive effects on your life.

6. Go back to the exercises in the book that you may not have done, and the questions that you did not answer in writing—for example, in the themes chapter, or even in the sixteen questions in Chapter 3. Take one at a time, and work your way through them over a few weeks. For example, did you take time to do the exercise where you scour your day looking for blessings (15) and reflecting on them using the *examen* method?

7. Discuss the questions with others. This can increase spiritual experiences as well as take our relationships to a deeper level. We can inspire others and be inspired by them, while becoming aware

of our experiences in new ways as we communicate about them. If you already did some of this in the communication chapters (10 and 11), you could continue in that vein. If not, you could find one person you feel comfortable with and share the exercises in the book with him or her—a good friend, a mentor, a close family member, or someone you are close to in your religious community. Allow it to open up discussions between you. Remember to use the "Rules of the Game" (at the end of Chapter 10) in any discussion. One of the nice things about sharing is that, like exercise buddies, we can be mutually encouraging. Additionally, we can savor good news and experiences even more when we share them with others—even with strangers. This kind of sharing has also been shown to enhance the value of the experiences and strengthen both our connections with others and our internal resources.[2]

8. Read about the ordinary spiritual experiences of others. There is great material out there from the distant past, the spiritual classics, from a variety of cultures, religions, and secular sources, as well as from writers of our own age and culture. Some of the best descriptions are found in poetry. This can open you up to seeing more in your own life.

9. What places and people and kinds of settings were most associated with various spiritual experiences for you? One great way to begin to answer this question is to revisit the comments you wrote down for each question in Chapter 3 or the thoughts you had when answering the questions. If you can increase your exposure to the people, places, and environments that were most associated with various spiritual experiences, you may increase your chances of these experiences becoming more available to you. You might want to keep a running list of these to refer to and increase your exposure to them in your life.

10. When you are doing mundane things—cooking, cleaning, driving to work, riding on public transit, eating, and playing—

reflect on the questions themselves and see if any spiritual experiences are hidden in the mundane tasks of the day. We multitask all the time: multitasking with this kind of focus has the capacity to change the character of the activity.

Attention Is Powerful

As I mentioned in the introductory chapter, just answering the DSES questions with numbers and/or words can cause good changes to take place in your life. The scientific support described there can also be applied to the exercises above. They prime you to feel these sensations in your life, notice these things, draw your attention to them, when other things in life are clamoring for attention. They bring these experiences into focus, so that you notice them more clearly. We can take control of our attentional resources, paying more attention to those things that will truly enhance our lives, but that are often drowned out by less important details of life.

There is a great video on the Web demonstrating "attentional blindness," a phenomenon studied by cognitive scientists. A group of students are playing basketball. Midway through the video, a man in a gorilla suit walks into the middle of the group and beats his chest. Most people viewing the video before it became famous did not see the man in the gorilla suit at all. It was a very effective way to demonstrate to students in my classes how we miss seeing things that are important because our attention is directed elsewhere. This study has been replicated in many versions. We focus on some things and miss others. In this book and with this set of questions, I hope to enable you to see and experience some valuable and delightful things in life that are too often missed by us all.

Just filling in words describing old age can make us tend to walk more slowly when we leave a room to walk down the hall.[3] Smelling soap can make us more careful about picking up crumbs when we sit down in front of a messy cake.[4] When we are primed with exposure to a memory of a person who has been a source of strength and love for us, it can prompt us to act more compassionately.[5] These effects happen in experimental settings without people knowing why they are changing their behavior. These kinds of implicit effects on our behaviors happen in many ways. By drawing our attention to the experiences described in this book, we may influence our actions even if we're not actively aware of why that is happening. Actively paying attention to experiences of spiritual connection and the themes underlying them can allow those things to affect us as we go through our days.

We have some choice about what we pay attention to in our surroundings. Not all aspects of the here and now are similarly valuable to attend to. In this book, and with the sixteen questions, you have been directing your attention to transcendent relationships, to spiritual connection, to connection with the ground of being, to the "more than" under the surface of the ordinary. In the context of attending to the sixteen items more can come alive for you; you can wake up.

As I have written this book, articulating the themes and writing about the items, I have seen these issues increasingly coming into the foreground of my life and have observed changes in myself. The items and themes relating to connection and love have worked their way into my relationships with others as I have been articulating them more clearly. I find myself being more aware of my blessings, drawing strength from God, and feeling love that is there. Before starting this project, I knew the Daily Spiritual Experience questions well, but returning to specific items consciously and daily in the context of writing, as well as paying attention to them in the context of the themes, has enhanced the frequency and vibrancy of my sensations of the "more than."

Frequent reflection on the DSES questions also draws our attention to small positive things in life. A study by economists reported that frequent small positive experiences and actions can cumulatively offset some of the big things that drag us down.[6] So shifting focus from major events to these small but good experiences can significantly improve our overall well-being.

Finally, remember the value of writing about your experiences in addition to just recalling them. As we saw in the introductory chapter, writing about things—that is, expression in words—has power as well; that has been demonstrated scientifically. It is worth taking time to reflect on your experiences, putting them into words, writing about them, and sharing them with others.[7]

The Role of Community in Awareness and Spiritual Connection

To keep up our awareness of spiritual experiences, it also helps to be nested in a community that supports that effort and one that encourages our vision to see the "more than."

Community can be temporary—for example, attending a music concert, participating in a protest march, being in a worship service, or participating in a wedding celebration. Alternatively, community may be longer lasting, with greater commitment to and deeper understanding of each other. It can even stretch back in time. Think of the "communion of saints," or connection to ancestors in indigenous traditions, or relationships to prophets and wise teachers in the past, or feeling a link to our great-grandparents or country of origin or others in our families who have died. Community does not require physical presence. We can be part of an Internet community or a scholarly community or a faith community, or feel connected to those struggling and suffering far away.

Not all relationships and communities enhance our connection with the transcendent or the flow of divine love. We can be stuck in relationships that we do not want to be in, or the community may be bound only by superficial social obligations. On the other hand, communities and relationships can provide opportunities for receiving and expressing love in ways that draw our attention to the divine in our lives. A doctor from India approached me during the coffee break at a meeting, bowed to me, and said "Namaste." He then explained that *Namaste* means "I greet the divine in you." This was a while ago, before the term had permeated popular culture, and his greeting and explanation touched me in a way that changed how I saw relationships.

The derivation of the word *religion* comes from the root *ligare*, to connect. Ideally, religious community represents people connected with each other and to a transcendent reality, and is often based on a basic set of principles and practices, ways of behaving and being. The community of people who attend a local church, synagogue, temple, or mosque can provide a special kind of environment for connection, where we can support and encourage each other in the context of a divine reality that can put the practical details of daily life in perspective. Many have a solid and good connection with a religious community already, one that sustains and encourages spiritual connection for them. If that is the case for you, great. But membership in a religious community is often not comfortable or congenial, and this is not made any easier by the failures of groups of people to realize their higher aspirations. Organizations are made up of flawed people with mixed motives. Some of us have been harmed by the attitudes or actions of those who profess a religious belief. Arrogance and hypocrisy are rife in all our institutions, and religious ones are no exception.

Although the religion of your upbringing or local culture may be a good place to start, many who have had a bad experience with religion when growing up need to rely on the resources of other traditions as they seek out a religious community of encouragement.

What community activities most encourage your connection with the divine, God, the transcendent? Music? Practical activities? Volunteering? Family events? Ones with strangers? Liturgy and ritual? Teachings and religious scriptures? No religious organization or group is going to fulfill all your desires in this area, but some will be better than others. Find one that you think will encourage the connection with God or the divine as described in other words for you, or approach the community you already relate to in a fresh way.

I visited Einstein's house in Bern, and I purchased a card there with his words:

> The positive development of a society in the absence of creative, independent-thinking, critical individuals is as inconceivable as the development of an individual in the absence of the stimulus of the community.

Let's Continue to Be Practical

Staying in touch with what is real is practical. We make decisions and act each day based on reality. As we live life in all its complexity, being in touch with reality helps us discover which goals are worth pursuing, and then prioritizing and sorting. We don't want to go through life with our eyes half-shut, but rather with them fully open.

One of the provisional titles I had for this book while writing it was *Tasting What's Real*. Hopefully, you are already finding more experiences in your daily life that enable you to touch and taste all that is real in life, both the surface real and the deeper, more transcendent real. Tables and chairs are real, atomic particles are real, our feelings are real, and our ordinary experiences of awe and beauty and divine connection are also real. Science provides us with ways of finding out more about reality. Our own direct experience, when honed and clear and open, provides us with another. These can complement one another as we move through our days.

The pragmatic William James wrote,

> [The] unseen region in question is not merely ideal, for it produces effects in this world. When we commune with it, work is actually done upon our finite personality, for we are turned into new men, and consequences in the way of conduct follow in the natural world upon our regenerative charge. But that which produces effects within another reality must be termed a reality itself.[8]

His comments support how practical it can be to pay attention to Daily Spiritual Experiences in our lives. The scores on the questions are linked with all sorts of other things in life (remember "Studies Have Shown," Chapter 5); this also points to their practical nature. By paying attention to the experiences and the themes that run through them, we attend to something that has practical importance. In doing so, we direct our attention to the "more than" in the midst of ordinary days.

Of course, you will continue to pay attention to the phone ringing, the text messages coming in with beeps, the small and big demands of your busy life. But by continuing to use the DSES questions and your verbal answers and number scores, you can better sift through and find what is important in your daily life, giving proper weight to the place of the "more than."[9] We do not want what appears to be urgent to drive out what is really important. What is really important to you, to me, to us, as we move through our days? And how does that influence what you do, how you respond, where you spend your precious time?

Henry James, the nineteenth-century novelist, wrote,

> Experience is never limited, and it is never complete; it is an immense sensibility; a kind of huge spider-web of the finest silken threads suspended in the chamber of consciousness, and catching every airborne particle in its tissue.[10]

We want to catch the numinous, the glorious, in the silken threads of our consciousness.

Science as a Tool for Spiritual Growth, Communication, and Personal Insight

In this book you have used a scientific tool to explore spiritual experience. That tool sprang from the way people like you, me, and others all over the world described their experiences, as well as from theoretical foundations and scientific research. As you have responded to the questions in the book, you have described and explored *your* particular experiences, which are unique. The development of the sixteen questions and the subsequent research on the scale established that the DSES is valid, according to the scientific method. In this way, the questions identify how your uniqueness may connect with that of others, discovering and building on things you may have in common as well as helping you to communicate your uniqueness in understandable ways.

Can we also think of the scientific method as a kind of spiritual practice? If you make the DSES part of your own life, using the numbers to track things, you are being a scientist. Practicing science in this way allows you to "stand outside yourself" and helps you cultivate objectivity about your own experiences and those of others by observing without judging. This provides useful distance. But remember the limits of numbers.

Sir Terry Pratchett, in one of his *Discworld* novels, describes a group of "auditors" of the universe, who think that uncertainty or chaos is unacceptable and therefore try to get rid of the messy humans. Rules drive the auditors—they are comfortable with rules. They are disembodied creatures in gray cloaks. As they try to take control, they end up assuming human form and, as such, are forced to better understand humans. In an attempt to understand why a painting is beautiful, they take chips of paint off a large work of art, sorting the paint chips into many same-colored piles.[11] To me this epitomizes why we need more than the scientific method. We need to adopt a playful attitude toward numbers and scientific results, not giving them more weight than they deserve. If you find that using the DSES's number scores takes you too much in the direction of the auditors, drop this approach and rely more on qualitative answers to the questions in the scale, questions sprinkled throughout this book, or comments that have particularly provoked a response in you. We need to see the "painting" as a whole to appreciate the beauty and mystery of our lives.

Continuing to Use This Book

One goal of this book is to enhance your capacity to experience spiritual connection and the flow of love in your life. Another is to enable you to communicate better with others about Daily

Spiritual Experiences and cultivate your mutual understanding. You have already done this to a certain extent if you have read through this book. Hopefully, you did some of the suggested activities and noted others for follow-up. Let's summarize a few of these that you have done and can continue to do:

1. Recording notes of your experiences for each of the questions in Chapter 3.
2. Answering the set of questions by giving yourself a number score for each question and a total average score. You may have already done this more than once over the course of this book and seen changes from your baseline score. Reflect on the implications of your answers for your life.
3. Doing the exercises in Chapters 6 through 9 (the themes chapters), and reexamining your experience through the lenses of the themes. You might even have identified subgroups of questions in these themes that you wish to follow more closely, like "love in" and "love out."
4. Communicating with others using the questions, if you feel comfortable doing this.
5. Practicing attentiveness and enhancing your sensitivity.
6. Using the website for this book, www.spiritualconnectionindailylife.com, to find resources.

You can decide how you will integrate the ideas and exercises from this book into the texture of your daily life. Even without diligently following the structure, revisiting the ideas will draw your attention to them. And you will find additional resources that will enrich this integration.

As Douglas Adams, author of *The Hitchhiker's Guide to the Galaxy*, wrote, "I rarely end up where I was intending to go, but often I end up somewhere I needed to be."[12]

Springing Forward

For me, one key question is this: Have I left space for the "more than" in my busy life? Have you? Boris Pasternak, the Russian novelist and poet, wrote, "Be alive, alive your full share, alive until the end."[13] Although this is the end of this book, this is not the end for you and me. From the depths of my heart, I wish joy for you as you continue to live your wild and wonderful life today, tomorrow, and the days after that.

Acknowledgments

I would like to thank those who helped in the birth of this book, including all my family and friends. I have experienced divine love directly and through many people—without that love this book would never have happened. All those who took time to discuss the DSES questions with me and share their experiences have contributed so much to the development of the DSES and this book. My appreciation goes out to the Abbey of Gethsemani for the hospitality during times on retreat during many years while the book was gestating, and particularly to Abbots Timothy and Damien for their permission to interview the monks. The e-mails and encouragement from those using the DSES have also kept me going. Rosemary Watkins, Carol Hoover, Jane Morris, and my daughter Anna took time to read the book in detail and gave valuable feedback. I especially thank Eric, my friend and husband, for his help with many practical details such as editing and website development, but even more for his encouragement, love, and support throughout the process.

APPENDIX

The Daily Spiritual Experience Questions

The list that follows includes items you may or may not experience.[1] Please consider how often you directly have this experience, and try to disregard whether you feel you should or should not have these experiences. A number of items use the word *God*. If this word is not a comfortable one for you, please substitute another word that calls to mind the divine or holy for you.

Response categories for all questions except number 4:
Never (1), Once in a while (2), Some days (3),
Most days (4), Every day (5), Many times a day (6)

___ 1. I am spiritually touched by the beauty of creation.

___ 2. I feel God's presence. (I feel the presence of the divine or holy.)

___ 3. I experience a connection to all of life.

___ 4. How close do you feel to God? (How close do you feel to the divine or holy?)
Not close (1), somewhat close (3), very close (5), as close as possible (6)

___ 5. I desire to be closer to God or in union with the divine.

___ 6. I feel God's love for me directly. (I feel divine love for me directly.)

___ 7. I feel God's love for me through others. (I feel divine love for me through others.)

___ 8. I feel a selfless caring for others.

___ 9. I accept others even when they do things I think are wrong.

___10. I find strength in my religion or spirituality.

___11. I find comfort in my religion or spirituality.

___12. I feel guided by God in the midst of daily activities. (I feel divine guidance in the midst of daily activities.)

___13. I ask for God's help in the midst of daily activities. (I ask for help from a higher power as I go through the day.)

___14. During worship, or at other times when connecting with God, I feel joy that lifts me out of my daily concerns. (I feel joy that lifts me out of my daily concerns when I experience connection with the divine or holy.)

___15. I feel thankful for my blessings.

___16. I feel deep inner peace or harmony.

_____

_____Total score

_____Total average (divide by 16)

Notes

INVITATION AND INTRODUCTION

1. Christian Wiman, "Hive of Nerves," *American Scholar*, Summer 2010, theamericanscholar.org.
2. E. L. Garland, B. Fredrickson, A. M. Kring, D. P. Johnson, P. S. Meyer, and D. L. Penn, "Upward Spirals of Positive Emotions Counter Downward Spirals of Negativity: Insights from the Broaden-and-Build Theory and Affective Neuroscience on the Treatment of Emotion Dysfunctions and Deficits in Psychopathology," *Clinical Psychology Review* 30, no. 7 (2010): 849–64.
3. R. M. Todd, W. A. Cunningham, A. K. Anderson, and E. Thompson, "Affect-Biased Attention as Emotion Regulation," *Trends in Cognitive Sciences* 16, no. 7 (2012): 365–72.
4. A. Dijksterhuis, P. K. Smith, R. B. van Baaren, and D. H. J. Wigboldus, "The Unconscious Consumer: Effects of Environment on Consumer Behavior," *Journal of Consumer Psychology* 15, no. 3 (2005): 193–202.
5. J. W. Pennebaker, "Theories, Therapies, and Taxpayers: On the Complexities of the Expressive Writing Paradigm," *Clinical Psychology: Science and Practice* 11, no. 2 (2004): 138–42; J. M. Smyth, A. A. Stone, A. Hurewitz, and A. Kaell, "Effects of Writing about Stressful Experiences on Symptom Reduction in Patients with Asthma or Rheumatoid Arthritis: A Randomized Trial," *JAMA* 281, no. 14 (1999): 1304–9.
6. M. D. Lieberman, N. I. Eisenberger, M. J. Crockett, S. M. Tom, J. H. Pfeifer, and B. M. Way, "Putting Feelings into Words: Affect Labeling Disrupts Amygdala Activity to Affective Stimuli," *Psychological Science* 18, no. 5 (2007): 421–28.
7. J. Quoidbach, E. V. Berry, M. Hansenne, and M. Mikolajczak, "Positive Emotion Regulation and Well-Being: Comparing the Impact of Eight Savoring and Dampening Strategies," *Personality and Individual Differences* 49, no. 5 (2010): 368–73.
8. D. D. Danner, D. Snowdon, and W. V. Friesen, "Positive Emotions in Early Life and Longevity: Findings from the Nun Study," *Journal of Personality and Social Psychology* 80, no. 5 (2001): 804–13.
9. Seamus Heaney, *The Human Chain* (London: Faber, 2010), 3.

CHAPTER 2: INSTRUCTIONS FOR ANSWERING
THE SIXTEEN QUESTIONS

1. Kamilla Venner, University of New Mexico, personal communication, May 17, 2010.
2. M. Dean, "Islam and Psychosocial Wellness in an American Afghan Refugee

Community," PhD dissertation, Curtin University, Centre for International Health, 2006.

3. K. Goggin, T. Murray, V. Malcarne, K. Metcalf, and M. Gerkovich, "What's God Got to Do with It? Adolescents' Beliefs about God's Role in Their Alcohol Use." Presented at the Twenty-Sixth Annual Scientific Meeting of the Research Society on Alcoholism, Fort Lauderdale, Florida, June 2003.

4. J. W. Pennebaker, "Writing about Emotional Experiences as a Therapeutic Process," *Psychological Science* 8, no. 3 (1997): 162–66.

5. J. M. Smyth, A. A. Stone, A. Hurewitz, and A. Kaell, "Effects of Writing about Stressful Experiences on Symptom Reduction in Patients with Asthma or Rheumatoid Arthritis: A Randomized Trial," *JAMA* 281, no. 14 (1999): 1304–9.

6. Chad Burton and Laura King, "The Health Benefits of Writing about Intensely Positive Experiences," *Journal of Research in Personality* 38, no. 2 (2004): 150–63.

CHAPTER 3: THE DAILY SPIRITUAL EXPERIENCE QUESTIONS

1. http://hubblesite.org/gallery/wallpaper/pr2005037a/.

2. Seamus Heaney, "Postscript," in *The Spirit Level* (New York: Farrar, Straus, Giroux, 1996), 82.

3. Some of the sixteen questions contain the word *God*. For each of these I am giving an alternate option written out here, but you may wish to substitute Allah, G-d, higher power, or some other word or phrase that calls to mind the transcendent for you.

4. http://nobelists.net/.

5. Dorianne Laux, *What We Carry* (Brockport, NY: BOA Editions, 1994).

6. William Wordsworth, *Lyrical Ballads* (London: J. & A. Arch, 1798).

7. Sharon Begley, "Science Finds God," *Newsweek*, July 27, 1998, 47.

8. K. Tippett, *On Being*, NPR, December 30, 2010.

9. Stevie Smith, "God the Eater," in *New Selected Poems of Stevie Smith* (New York: New Directions, 1988), 80.

10. http://www.joepugmusic.com/video/, Hymn 101.

11. John S. Rigden, *Rabi: Scientist and Citizen* (New York: Basic Books, 1987), reissued with a new preface (Cambridge, MA: Harvard University Press, 2000), 73.

12. S. Cohen, L. Underwood, and B. Gottlieb, eds., *Social Support Measurement and Interventions: A Guide for Health and Social Scientists* (New York: Oxford University Press, 2000).

13. Jawid Mojaddedi, Andrew Rippin, and Norman Calder, *Classical Islam: A Sourcebook of Religious Literature* (London: Taylor and Francis, 2004).

14. Rumi, "Some Kiss We Want," from *The Soul of Rumi: A New Collection of Ecstatic Poems*, trans. Coleman Barks (New York: HarperOne, 2002), 125.

15. Song of Songs 2:13–14 NIV.

16. Charles Addams, *New Yorker*, February 16, 1981, cover.

17. Rabindranath Tagore, *Poetry*, February 2012, 419.

18. 1 Corinthians 13:4–8 NIV.

19. William Shakespeare, *The Merchant of Venice*, 4.1.184–87.

20. L. A. Neff and B. R. Karney, "Compassionate Love in Early Marriage," in *The Science of Compassionate Love: Theory, Research, and Applications*, ed. B. Fehr, S.

Sprecher, and L. G. Underwood (Oxford: Wiley-Blackwell, 2009). The selfless caring and the accept others questions were used in this study.

21. L. G. Underwood, "Interviews with Trappist Monks as a Contribution to Research Methodology in the Investigation of Compassionate Love," *Journal for the Theory of Social Behavior* 35, no. 3 (September 2005): 285–302.

22. Rainer Maria Rilke, trans. Eric Beversluis, "Gott spricht zu jedem nur, eh er ihn macht" in *Das Stunden-Buch*, 2nd ed., (Leipzig: Insel-Verlag, 1907).

23. J. Carmody, "The Case: Bad Care, Good Care, and Spiritual Preservations," *Second Opinion* 20, no. 1 (1994): 35–39.

24. R. S. Friedman, "Re-Exploring the Connection between Terror Management Theory and Dissonance Theory," *Personality and Social Psychology Bulletin* 31, no. 9 (2005): 1217–25.

25. Julian of Norwich, *Showings*, trans. James Walsh (Mahwah, NJ: Paulist Press, 1978), 52.

26. *The Way of the Pilgrim, and The Pilgrim Continues His Way*, trans. Helen Bacovcin (New York: Image Books, 1992), 177.

27. Thomas Merton, *The Way of Chuang Tzu* (New York: New Directions, 1965).

28. John Cassian, *Conferences/John Cassian* (New York: Paulist Press, 1985).

29. C. S. Lewis, *Mere Christianity* (New York: Macmillan, 1952).

30. http://www.youtube.com/watch?v=JQRRnAhmB58. This has a special resonance with me as I spent a particularly tough time of my life living in urban Oakland.

31. R. Emmons and M. E. McCullough, "Counting Blessings versus Burdens: An Experimental Investigation of Gratitude and Subjective Well-Being in Daily Life," *Journal of Personality and Social Psychology* 84, no. 2 (2003): 377–89.

32. William Stafford, "Any Morning," in *Ohio Review*, Volume 50 (1993).

33. Søren Kierkegaard, *Journals* IV A 164 (1843).

34. M.-A. Bruno, J. L. Bernheim, D. Ledoux, F. Pellas, A. Demertzi, and S. Laureys, "A Survey on Self-Assessed Well-Being in a Cohort of Chronic Locked-in Syndrome Patients: Happy Majority, Miserable Minority," *BMJ Open* 2011;1:e000039 doi:10.1136/bmjopen-2010-000039.

CHAPTER 4: USING THE NUMBER SCORES

1. L. G. Underwood, "Ordinary Spiritual Experience: Qualitative Research, Interpretive Guidelines, and Population Distribution for the Daily Spiritual Experience Scale," *Archive for the Psychology of Religion/Archiv für Religionspsychologie* 28, no. 1 (2006): 181–218; C. G. Ellison and D. Fan, "Daily Spiritual Experiences and Psychological Well-Being among US Adults," *Social Indicators Research* 88 (2008): 247–71.

2. www.dsescale.org.

CHAPTER 5: "STUDIES HAVE SHOWN"

1. For more details on specific references to studies not explicitly cited, see Lynn G. Underwood, "The Daily Spiritual Experience Scale: Overview and Results," *Religions* 2, no. 1 (2011): 29–50, http://www.mdpi.com/2077-1444/2/1/29/.

2. N. Maisel, A. Rauer, G. Marshall, and B. R. Karney, "Social Support after a Partner's Traumatic Injury: Situational, Relationship, and Individual Difference

Predictors," in *Support Processes in Intimate Relationships*, ed. K. Sullivan and J. Davila (New York: Oxford University Press, 2010), 264–88.

3. D. E. Bell Jr., "The Relationship between Distal Religious and Proximal Spiritual Variables and Self-Reported Marital Happiness," PhD dissertation, Florida State University College of Medicine, 2000.

4. F. D. Fincham, C. Ajayi, and S. R. H. Beach, "Spirituality and Marital Satisfaction in African American Couples," *Psychology of Religion and Spirituality* 3, no. 4 (2011): 259–68.

5. S. Kalkstein and R. B. Tower, "The Daily Spiritual Experiences Scale and Well-Being: Demographic Comparisons and Scale Validation with Older Jewish Adults and a Diverse Internet Sample," *Journal of Religion and Health* 48, no. 4 (2009): 402–17.

6. K. Skarupski, G. Fitchett, D. Evans, and C. F. Mendes, "Daily Spiritual Experiences in a Biracial Community-Based Population of Older Adults," *Aging and Mental Health* 14, no. 7 (2010): 779–89.

7. L. Easterling, L. Gamino, K. W. Sewell, and L. S. Stirman, "Spiritual Experience, Church Attendance, and Bereavement," *Journal of Pastoral Care* 54, no. 3 (2000): 263–75.

8. C. G. Ellison, A. K. Henderson, and T. Moore, "Daily Spiritual Experiences, Prosocial Attitudes, and Helping Behaviors among U.S. Adults," Paper presented at annual meetings of the Society for the Scientific Study of Religion, Phoenix, November 9–11, 2012.

9. C. Einolf, "Daily Spiritual Experiences and Prosocial Behavior," *Social Indicators Research* (2011), DOI 10.1007/s1 1205-011-9917-3.

10. R. Duffy, "Spirituality, Religion, and Work Values," *Journal of Psychology and Theology* 38, no. 1 (2010): 1–17.

11. C. J. Van Dyke, D. Glenwick, J. Cecero, and S. K. Kim, "The Relationship of Religious Coping and Spirituality to Adjustment and Psychological Distress in Urban Early Adolescents," *Mental Health, Religion, and Culture* 12, no. 4(2009): 369–83.

12. A. Desrosiers and L. Miller, "Relational Spirituality and Depression in Adolescent Girls," *Journal of Clinical Psychology* 63, no. 10 (2007): 1021–37.

13. E. G. M. Sanchez, F. A. L. Arocena, and J. C. M. Ceballos, "Daily Spiritual Experience in Basques and Mexicans: A Quantitative Study," *Journal of Transpersonal Research* 2 (2010): 10–25.

14. S. M. Ng et al., "Validation of the Chinese Version of Underwood's Daily Spiritual Experience Scale: Transcending Cultural Boundaries?" *International Journal of Behavioral Medicine* 16, no. 2 (2009): 91–97.

15. E. Voltmer, A. Büssing, C. Thomas, and C. Spahn, "Religiosität, Spiritualität, Gesundheit und Berufsbezogene Verhaltensmuster bei Pastoren zweier freikirchlich-protestantischer Denominationen/Religiosity" (Spirituality, Health, and Work-Related Behavior Patterns in Pastors of Two Free Protestant Denominations), *Psychotherapie Psychosomatik Medizinische Psychologie* 60, no. 11 (2010): 425–33.

16. J. M. Holland and R. A. Neimeyer, "Reducing the Risk of Burnout in End-of-Life Care Settings: The Role of Daily Spiritual Experiences and Training," *Palliative and Supportive Care* 3, no. 3 (2005): 173–81.

17. H. T. Ayo, S. H. Agofure, and K. Adebukola, "Psychosocial Variables as Predictors of Work Family Conflict among Secondary School Teachers in Irele Local

Government Area, Ondo State, Nigeria," *Pakistan Journal of Social Sciences* 6, no. 1 (2009): 11–18.

18. G. Woods, "The 'Bigger Feeling': The Importance of Spiritual Experience in Educational Leadership," *Education Management Administration and Leadership* 35, no. 1 (2007): 135–55.

19. J. M. Sprung, M. T. Sliter, and S. M. Jex, "Spirituality as a Moderator of the Relationship between Workplace Aggression and Employee Outcomes," *Personality and Individual Differences* 53, no. 7 (2012): 930–34.

20. M. T. Green, P. Duncan, and S. A. Kodatt, "The Relationship between Follower Ratings of Leadership and the Leaders' Spirituality," *Journal of Spirituality, Leadership and Management* 5, no. 1 (2011): 46–57.

21. S. Roberts and T. Jarrett, "Are Spiritual People Really Less Evil? A Study Exploring the Influence of Spirituality on Deviance in the Workplace." Presentation at the Midwest Academy of Management Fifty-Fourth Annual Conference, Omaha, Nebraska, October 20–22, 2011.

22. C. L. Park, D. Edmondson, A. Hale-Smith, and T. O. Blank, "Religiousness/ Spirituality and Health Behaviors in Younger Adult Cancer Survivors: Does Faith Promote a Healthier Lifestyle?" *Journal of Behavioral Medicine* 32, no. 6 (2009): 582–91.

23. C. L. Park, M. Brooks, and J. Sussman, "Dimensions of Religion and Spirituality in Psychological Adjustment in Older Adults Living with Congestive Heart Failure," in *Faith and Well-being in Later Life: Linking Theory with Evidence in an Interdisciplinary Inquiry*, ed. A. Ai and M. Ardelt (Hauppauge, NY: Nova Science, 2009), 41–58.

24. M. L. Fitzgibbon et al., "Results of a Faith-Based Weight Loss Intervention for Black Women," *Journal of the National Medical Association* 97, no. 10 (2005): 1393–402.

25. Aiste Pranckeviciene, Egidija Zasytyte, and Loreta Gustainiene, "Relationship between Spirituality and Wellness in a Sample of University Students," *International Journal of Psychology: A Biopsychosocial Approach* 2 (2008): 1–2, psyjournal.vdu.lt.

26. A. K. Wutoh, G. N. English, M. Daniel, K. A. Kendall, E. K. Cobran, V. C. Tasker, G. Hodges et al., "Pilot Study to Assess HIV Knowledge, Spirituality, and Risk Behaviors among Older African Americans," *Journal of the National Medical Association* 103, no. 3 (March 2011): 265–68.

27. H. G. Koenig, L. K. George, P. Titus, and K. G. Meador, "Religion, Spirituality, and Acute Care Hospitalization and Long-Term Care by Older Patients," *Archives of Internal Medicine* 164, no. 14 (2004): 1579–85.

28. K. Skarupski, G. Fitchett, D. Evans, and C. F. Mendes, "Daily Spiritual Experiences in a Biracial Community-Based Population of Older Adults," *Aging and Mental Health* 14, no. 7 (2010): 779–89.

29. J. Maselko and L. D. Kubzansky, "Gender Differences in Religious Practices, Spiritual Experiences, and Health: Results from the US General Social Survey," *Social Science and Medicine* 62, no. 11 (2006): 2848–60.

30. N. Bailly and N. Roussiau, "The Daily Spiritual Experience Scale (DSES): Validation of the Short Form in an Elderly French Population," *Canadian Journal on Aging/La Revue Canadienne du Vieillissement* 29, no. 2 (2010): 223–31.

31. F. J. Keefe, G. Affleck, J. Lefebvre, L. Underwood, D. S. Caldwell, J. Drew, J. Egert, J. Gibson, and K. Pargament, "Living with Rheumatoid Arthritis: The

Role of Daily Spirituality and Daily Religious and Spiritual Coping," *Journal of Pain* 2, no. 2 (2001): 101–10.

32. A. B. Wachholtz and K. I. Pargament, "Is Spirituality a Critical Ingredient of Meditation? Comparing the Effects of Spiritual Meditation, Secular Meditation, and Relaxation on Spiritual, Psychological, Cardiac, and Pain Outcomes," *Journal of Behavioral Medicine* 28, no. 4 (2005): 369–84.

33. A. E. Rippentrop, E. M. Altmaier, and J. J. Chen, "The Relationship between Religion/Spirituality and Physical Health, Mental Health, and Pain in a Chronic Pain Population," *Pain* 116, no. 3 (2005): 311–21.

34. E. Robinson, J. Cranford, J. Webb, and K. Brower, "Six-Month Changes in Spirituality, Religiousness, and Heavy Drinking in a Treatment-Seeking Sample," *Journal of Studies on Alcohol and Drugs* 68, no. 2 (2007): 282–90.

35. I. Parhami, M. Davtian, M. Collard, J. Lopez, and T. W. Fong, "A Preliminary 6-Month Prospective Study Examining Self-Reported Religious Preference, Religiosity/Spirituality, and Retention at a Jewish Residential Treatment Center for Substance-Related Disorders," *Journal of Behavioral Health Services and Research* (2005), doi:10.1007/s11414-012-9279-x.

36. S. E. Zemore and L. A. Kaskutas, "Helping, Spirituality, and Alcoholics Anonymous in Recovery," *Journal of Studies on Alcohol* 65, no. 3 (2004): 383–91.

37. C. G. Ellison and D. Fan, "Daily Spiritual Experiences and Psychological Well-Being among US Adults," *Social Indicators Research* 88, no. 2 (2008): 247–71. General Social Survey is conducted by the University of Chicago and funded by the National Science Foundation and considered a gold standard survey.

38. L. G. Underwood, "The Daily Spiritual Experience Scale: Overview and Results," *Religions* 2, no. 1 (2011): 29–50.

39. J. W. Ciarrocchi and E. Deneke, "Happiness and the Varieties of Religious Experience: Religious Support, Practices, and Spirituality as Predictors of Well-Being," *Research in the Social Scientific Study of Religion* 15 (2005): 209–331; Ciarrocchi and Deneke, "Hope, Optimism, Pessimism, and Spirituality as Predictors of Wellbeing Controlling for Personality," *Research in the Social Scientific Study of Religion* 16 (2005): 161–83.

40. J. McCauley, M. J. Tarpley, S. Haaz, and S. J. Bartlett, "Daily Spiritual Experiences of Older Adults with and without Arthritis and the Relationship to Health Outcomes," *Arthritis and Rheumatism* 59, no. 1 (2008): 122–28.

41. C. J. Van Dyke, D. Glenwick, J. Cecero, and S. K. Kim, "The Relationship of Religious Coping and Spirituality to Adjustment and Psychological Distress in Urban Early Adolescents," *Mental Health, Religion, and Culture* 12, no. 4 (2009): 369–83.

42. E. G. M. Sanchez, F. A. L. Arocena, and J. C. M. Ceballos, "Daily Spiritual Experience in Basques and Mexicans: A Quantitative Study," *Journal of Transpersonal Research* 2 (2010): 10–25; L. G. Underwood and J. A. Teresi, "The Daily Spiritual Experience Scale: Development, Theoretical Description, Reliability, Exploratory Factor Analysis, and Preliminary Construct Validity Using Health-Related Data," *Annals of Behavioral Medicine* 24, no. 1 (2002): 22–33; A. Desrosiers and L. Miller, "Relational Spirituality and Depression in Adolescent Girls," *Journal of Clinical Psychology* 63 (2007): 1021–37; J. A. Blumenthal, M. A. Babyak, G. Ironson, C. Thorensen, L. Powell, S. Czajkowski, M. Burg, F. J. Keefe, P. Steffen, and D. Catellier, "Spirituality, Religion, and Clinical Outcomes in Patients Recovering from an Acute Myocardial Infarction,"

Psychosomatic Medicine 69, no. 6 (2007): 501–8; J. McCauley, M. J. Tarpley, S. Haaz, and S. J. Bartlett, "Daily Spiritual Experiences of Older Adults with and without Arthritis and the Relationship to Health Outcomes"; M. Mofidi, R. F. DeVellis, D. G. Blazer, B. M. DeVellis, A. T. Panter, and J. M. Jordan, "Spirituality and Depressive Symptoms in a Racially Diverse US Sample of Community-Dwelling Adults," *Journal of Nervous and Mental Disease* 194, no. 12 (2006): 975–77; H. G. Koenig, L. K. George, P. Titus, and K. G. Meador, "Religion, Spirituality, and Acute Care Hospitalization and Long-Term Care by Older Patients"; K. Skarupski, G. Fitchett, D. Evans, and C. F. Mendes, "Daily Spiritual Experiences in a Biracial Community-Based Population of Older Adults," *Aging and Mental Health* 14, no. 7 (2010): 779–89; S. Kalkstein and R. B. Tower, "The Daily Spiritual Experiences Scale and Well-Being: Demographic Comparisons and Scale Validation with Older Jewish Adults and a Diverse Internet Sample," *Journal of Religion and Health* 48, no. 4 (2009): 402–17; C. Watlington, "The Roles of Religion and Spirituality among African American Survivors of Domestic Violence," *Journal of Clinical Psychology* 62, no. 7 (2006): 837–57.

43. S. Tsabary, "The Influences of Gender, Parenthood, and Spiritual Experiences on Depressive Symptoms," PhD thesis, Columbia University, 2008.

44. S. H. Ballew, S. M. Hannum, J. M. Gaines, K. A. Marx, and J. M. Parrish, "The Role of Spiritual Experiences and Activities in the Relationship between Chronic Illness and Psychological Well-Being," *Journal of Religion and Health* 51, no. 4 (December 2012): 1386–96.

45. J. Han and V. Richardson, "The Relationship between Depression and Loneliness among Homebound Older Persons: Does Spirituality Moderate This Relationship?" *Journal of Religion and Spirituality in Social Work: SOCIAL THOUGHT* 29, no. 3 (2010): 218–36.

46. J. Park and S. Roh, "Daily Spiritual Experiences, Social Support, and Depression among Elderly Korean Immigrants," *Aging & Mental Health*, DOI:10.1080/13607863.2012.715138.

47. S. Kalkstein and R. B. Tower, "The Daily Spiritual Experiences Scale and Well-Being: Demographic Comparisons and Scale Validation with Older Jewish Adults and a Diverse Internet Sample," *Journal of Religion and Health* 48, no. 4 (2009): 402–17; E. G. M. Sanchez, F. A. L. Arocena, and J. C. M. Ceballos, "Daily Spiritual Experience in Basques and Mexicans: A Quantitative Study"; L. G. Underwood and J. A. Teresi, "The Daily Spiritual Experience Scale: Development, Theoretical Description, Reliability, Exploratory Factor Analysis, and Preliminary Construct Validity Using Health-Related Data."

48. B. R. Jackson, "Daily Spiritual Experiences: A Buffer Against the Effect of Daily Perceived Stress on Daily Mood," master's thesis, Notre Dame University, 2010.

49. K. Rounding, K. E. Hart, S. Hibbard, and M. Carroll, "Emotional Resilience in Young Adults Who Were Reared by Depressed Parents: The Moderating Effects of Offspring Religiosity/Spirituality," *Journal of Spirituality in Mental Health* 13, no. 4 (2011): 236–46.

50. J. M. Currier, J. Mallot, T. E. Martinez, C. Sandy, and R. A. Neimeyer, "Bereavement, Religion, and Posttraumatic Growth: A Matched Control Group Investigation," *Psychology of Religion and Spirituality* (2012), doi:10.1037/a0027708.

51. P. S. Bay, S. S. Ivy, and C. L. Terry, "The Effect of Spiritual Retreat on Nurses'

Spirituality: A Randomized Controlled Study," *Holistic Nursing Practice* 24, no. 3 (2010): 125–33.

52. P. A. Boelens, R. R. Reeves, W. H. Replogle, and H. G. Koenig, "A Randomized Trial of the Effect of Prayer on Depression and Anxiety," *International Journal of Psychiatry in Medicine* 39, no. 4 (2009): 377–92.

53. W. R. Miller, A. Forcehimes, M. J. O'Leary, and M. D. LaNoue, "Spiritual Direction in Addiction Treatment: Two Clinical Trials," *Journal of Substance Abuse Treatment* 35, no. 4 (2008): 434–42.

54. E. D. Goldstein, "Sacred Moments: Implications on Well-Being and Stress," *Journal of Clinical Psychology* 63, no. 10 (2007): 1001–9.

55. Cara Geary and Susan L. Rosenthal, "Sustained Impact of MBSR on Stress, Well-Being, and Daily Spiritual Experiences for 1 Year in Academic Health Care Employees," *Journal of Alternative and Complementary Medicine* 17, no. 10 (October 2011): 939–44.

56. Janet R. Weber and Jane Kelley Lippincott, "Health Assessment in Nursing," 2009 IN-CAM Outcomes Database, outcomesdatabase.org/.

57. S. F. Dailey, J. R. Curry, M. C. Harper, H. J. Hartwig Moorhead, and C. S. Gill, "Exploring the Spiritual Domain: Tools for Integrating Spirituality and Religion in Counseling," 2011, http://counselingoutfitters.com/.

PART FOUR: THEMES

1. P. H. Thibodeau and L. Boroditsky, "Metaphors We Think With: The Role of Metaphor in Reasoning," *PLoS ONE* 6, no. 2 (2011). *PLoS ONE* 6(2): e16782. doi:10.1371/journal.pone.0016782.

CHAPTER 6: THE FLOW OF LOVE

1. L. G. Underwood, "Interviews with Trappist Monks as a Contribution to Research Methodology in the Investigation of Compassionate Love," *Journal for the Theory of Social Behavior* 35, no. 3 (September 2005): 285–302.

2. L. G. Underwood, "Compassionate Love: A Framework for Research," in *The Science of Compassionate Love: Theory, Research, and Applications*, ed. B. Fehr, S. Sprecher, and L. G. Underwood (Oxford: Wiley-Blackwell, 2009), 3–26.

3. B. Fehr, S. Sprecher, and L. G. Underwood, eds., *The Science of Compassionate Love: Theory, Research, and Applications* (Oxford: Wiley-Blackwell, 2009).

4. Lynn Underwood, "Compassionate Love," in *Encyclopedia of Bioethics*, 3rd ed., ed. Stephen G. Post (New York: Macmillan Reference USA, 2004), 483–88.

5. George Herbert, "Love (III)," in *Four Metaphysical Poets* (London: J. M. Dent, 1997), 37.

6. W. H. Auden, *Forewords and Afterwords*, selected by Edward Mendelson (New York: Random House, 1973), 69–70 (from lecture on Auden, see http://www.gresham.ac.uk/event.asp?PageId=45&EventId=820).

7. http://www.poetryarchive.org/poetryarchive/singlePoem.do?poemId=1396.

8. Jessica Powers, *Selected Poetry of Jessica Powers*, ed. Regina Siegfried and Robert Morneau (Kansas City, MO: Sheed and Ward, 1989), 1.

CHAPTER 7: CONNECTION VERSUS ALIENATION

1. http://www.youtube.com/watch?v=FxudKL1IB6U.
2. Ilia Delio, Keith Douglass Warner, and Pamela Wood, *Care for Creation: A Franciscan Spirituality of the Earth* (Cincinnati: St. Anthony Messenger Press, 2008).
3. P. Oliner, *Saving the Forsaken: Religious Culture and the Rescue of Jews in Nazi Europe* (New Haven, CT: Yale University Press, 2004).
4. U. Schjoedt et al., "Highly Religious Participants Recruit Areas of Social Cognition in Personal Prayer," *Social Cognitive and Affective Neuroscience* 4, no. 2 (2009): 199–207.
5. http://www.youtube.com/watch?v=K6u5D-5LWSg.
6. http://www.youtube.com/watch?v=l1BTWCpEFRQ, or the Taize version, http://www.youtube.com/watch?v=X9e_QO1ATho.
7. Billy Collins, *Picnic, Lightning* (Pittsburgh: University of Pittsburgh Press, 1998), 37.
8. Henri Nouwen and Phillip Roderick, *Beloved: Henri Nouwen in Conversation* (Grand Rapids: Eerdmans, 2007).
9. Seyyed Hossein Nasr, "We and You, Let Us Meet in God's Love," in a speech delivered at the "Common Word" meeting with Pope Benedict XVI, Nov. 6, 2008.
10. Phillip Shaver, Mario Mikulincer, and Omri Gillath, "A Behavioral Systems Perspective on Compassionate Love," in *The Science of Compassionate Love: Theory, Research, and Applications*, ed. B. Fehr, S. Sprecher, and L. G. Underwood (Oxford: Wiley-Blackwell, 2009), 225–56.
11. Patrick Kavanagh, *Collected Poems* (London: Allen Lane, 2004), 229.

CHAPTER 8: YES!

1. James Stephens, *Irish Fairy Stories* (Macmillan, 1923).
2. Anthony de Mello, *Sadhana, a Way to God: Christian Exercises in Eastern Form* (New York: Image, 1984), 140.
3. Dr. C. K. Hsee, a behavioral economist at the University of Chicago, has done a great selection of research projects on happiness, and discovered a number of things. First, it is better to invest in activities that we won't just adapt to over time (e.g., decreased commute time rather than larger home size). And second, to invest in things that are in and of themselves valuable to you, rather than comparatively so, can improve your happiness (e.g., heating rather than jewelry). He and others have also found that we are notoriously bad at predicting what will make us happy in the future; C. K. Hsee, F. Xu, and N. Tang, "Two Recommendations on the Pursuit of Happiness," *Science* 37, June (2008): 115–32.
4. P. Brickman, D. Coates, and R. Janoff-Bulman, "Lottery Winners and Accident Victims: Is Happiness Relative?" *Journal of Personality and Social Psychology* 36, no. 8 (1978): 917–27.
5. E. L. Garland et al., "Upward Spirals of Positive Emotions Counter Downward Spirals of Negativity: Insights from the Broaden-and-Build Theory and Affective Neuroscience on the Treatment of Emotion Dysfunctions and Defi-

cits in Psychopathology," *Clinical Psychology Review* 30, no. 7 (2010): 849–64; D. Mochon, M. I. Norton, and D. Ariely, "Getting off the Hedonic Treadmill, One Step at a Time: The Impact of Regular Religious Practice and Exercise on Well-Being," *Journal of Economic Psychology* 29, no. 5 (2008): 632–42.

6. Evelyn Underhill, *Practical Mysticism* (1915; Columbus, OH: Ariel Press, 1988).

7. William James, *The Varieties of Religious Experience*, (New York: Collier Macmillan, 1985), 49–50.

8. Wendell Berry, *The Collected Poems of Wendell Berry, 1957–1982* (New York: North Point Press, 1987).

CHAPTER 9: TRANSLATING "GOD"

1. Antony Flew, *There Is a God: How the World's Most Notorious Atheist Changed His Mind* (New York: HarperCollins, 2007), 101–3.

2. A. J. Heschel, *Man Is Not Alone: A Philosophy of Religion* (New York: Farrar Strauss and Young, 1951), 88.

3. Simone Weil, *Gravity and Grace* (London: Routledge, 1963), 132.

4. Tomáš Halík, *Night of the Confessor* (New York: Image, 2012), 115.

5. Heisenberg, as cited in Ulrich Hildebrand, "Das Universum - Hinweis auf Gott?" in *Ethos* no. 10 (Oktober 1988): 10.

6. Wendell Berry, *Farming: A Handbook* (New York: Harcourt Brace Jovanovich, 1971), 56.

7. http://www.youtube.com/watch?v=8BnFowzj9ckci.

8. Albert Einstein, *Ideas and Opinions*, trans. Sonja Bargmann (New York: Dell, 1973), 255.

CHAPTER 10: WHY AND HOW TO COMMUNICATE USING DAILY SPIRITUAL EXPERIENCES

1. Michael Morrison, Sarah Gan, Chris Dubelaar, Harmen Oppewal, "In-Store Music and Aroma Influences on Shopper Behavior and Satisfaction," *Journal of Business Research* 64, no. 6 (2011): 558–64; A. J. Healy, N. Malhotra, and C. H. Mo, "Irrelevant Events Affect Voters' Evaluations of Government Performance," *Proceedings of the National Academy of Sciences of the United States of America* 107, no. 29 (2010): 12804–9.

2. William James, *The Varieties of Religious Experience: A Study in Human Nature* (New York: Random House, 1902), 80.

3. G. M. Brelsford, S. Marinelli, J. W. Ciarrocchi, and G. S. Dy-Liacco, "Generativity and Spiritual Disclosure in Close Relationships," *Psychology of Religion and Spirituality* 1, no. 3 (2009): 150–61.

4. Czeslaw Milosz, *The Captive Mind*, trans. Jane Zielonko (1951; New York: Vintage Books, 1953), epigraph.

CHAPTER 11: ORGANIZATIONAL, PROFESSIONAL, AND PERSONAL USES

1. R. Duffy, "Spirituality, Religion, and Work Values," *Journal of Psychology and Theology* 38 (2010): 1–17.

2. L. Bouckaert, "Business and Spirituality in Europe," *Spiritus*, 11, no. 1 (2011): 24–37.
3. See Chapter 5, "Studies Have Shown."
4. Robert Kegan and Lisa Laskow Lahey, *Immunity to Change: How to Overcome It and Unlock the Potential in Yourself and Your Organization* (Cambridge, MA: Harvard Business School Press, 2009).
5. http://www.openculture.com/2012/03/david_foster_wallaces_kenyon _graduation_speech.html.
6. Jerald D. Gort, Hendrik M. Vroom, Rein Fernhout, and Anton Wessels, *On Sharing Religious Experience* (Grand Rapids: Eerdmans, 1992).
7. Samir Selmanovic, *It's Really All about God: How Islam, Atheism, and Judaism Made Me a Better Christian* (San Francisco: Jossey-Bass, 2009).

CHAPTER 12: WHAT NOW? WHAT NEXT?

1. Marcel Proust, *Le temps retrouvé* (1927; Paris: Gallimard, 1987), 424.
2. H. T. Reis, S. M. Smith, C. L. Carmichael, P. A. Caprariello, A. Rodrigues, and M. R Maniaci, "Are You Happy for Me ? How Sharing Positive Events With Others Provides Personal and Interpersonal Benefits," *Journal of Personality and Social Psychology*, 99, no. 2 (2010): 311–29.
3. A. Dijksterhuis, P. K. Smith, R. B. van Baaren, and D. H. J. Wigboldus, "The Unconscious Consumer: Effects of Environment on Consumer Behavior," *Journal of Consumer Psychology* 15, no. 3 (2005): 193–202.
4. R. W. Holland, M. Hendriks, and H. Aarts, "Smells Like Clean Spirit: Nonconscious Effects of Scent on Cognition and Behavior," *Psychological Science* 16, no. 9 (2005): 689–93.
5. M. Mikulincer and P. R. Shaver, "Attachment Security, Compassion, and Altruism," *Current Directions in Psychological Science* 14, no. 1 (2005): 34–38.
6. D. Mochon, M. I. Norton, and D. Ariely, "Getting Off the Hedonic Treadmill, One Step at a Time: The Impact of Regular Religious Practice and Exercise on Well-being," *Journal of Economic Psychology*, 29, no. 5 (2008): 632–42.
7. C. M. Burton and L. King, "Effects of (Very) Brief Writing on Health: The Two-Minute Miracle," *British Journal of Health Psychology* 13, part 1 (2008): 9–14.
8. William James, *The Varieties of Religious Experience: A Study in Human Nature* (1904; New York: Collier Macmillan, 1961), 399.
9. As Paul Éluard wrote, "Il y a un autre monde mais il est dans celui-ci" (There is another world, but it is in this one).
10. Henry James, *The Art of Fiction*, *Longman's Magazine* 4 (1884), 502–21.
11. Terry Pratchett, *Thief of Time: A Novel of Discworld* (New York: HarperCollins, 2001).
12. Douglas Adams, *The Long Dark Tea-Time of the Soul* (1905; New York: Pocket Books, Simon and Schuster, 1990), 153.
13. Boris Pasternak, "To Be Famous," in *Silver and Steel: Twentieth-Century Russian Poetry, An Anthology*, ed. Yevgeny Yevtushenko (New York: Doubleday, 1994), 213–14.

APPENDIX

1. This is a different order of the questions from that one used in research. The items have been reordered to reflect the order used in Chapter 3. The responses have been reversed, so that "Never" is now the first response and "Many times a day" is now the highest number. This makes it easier to refer to "high" and "low" scores in a nonconfusing manner, and most researchers transform the data in this way prior to evaluation. These subtle changes enhance your ability to personally use the scale effectively.